GET UNSTUCK

10 Tools of Wisdom that Help You Achieve
Greater Love, Energy, and Growth

Terry Belmont and Nina Engstrand

ISBN: 978-1-5136-2065-7

Disclaimer

Contents

Sending You Gratitude

Thank You so much for buying this book. As an expression of our gratitude, we would like to offer you "10 tips to raise your energy when feeling low" to download for FREE.

To Download:

theinvitationtochange.com/download

Introduction

Living a meaningful and happy life is so worth striving for. It's a life where we can be in balance with ourselves, embrace the present moment, and be excited about the future. However, we all go through times in our lives when we do not feel in tune with ourselves or others, when we feel frozen in an unwanted situation, when we just feel stuck. Are you feeling this way or even having grumblings that you might not be doing what you should? Are you wondering how you can pull yourself out of it? Or, do you have a friend in a difficult situation whom you would like to help?

There are so many ways you can get stuck — in a relationship, your career, your health, or even your mindset. But being stuck is not the problem. The problem is that you do not know how to move on and get unstuck. Based upon our own experience, our research, and our numerous discussions with others, we know that being stuck is a limiting factor in many people's lives. The reasons may be different from person to person, and the ways the feeling affects everyone is different. However, the ways how to get unstuck are similar.

This book makes the way to get unstuck clear, providing you with proven and actionable tools to find your own path in life.

No one can tell you when you are ready to get unstuck, but in this book you will learn how to make the necessary changes to reach the next level in your life.

We, Terry and Nina, met while walking the Camino de Santiago, also called The Way of St James. We will refer to this as "the camino." The camino is a 500-mile trail across northern Spain, which has been walked by pilgrims for over 1000 years. About a year before we met on the camino, we each, separately, realized that a major life change was necessary. Was every part of our lives stuck? No. However, some aspects of our lives were clearly not moving forward as we would have liked; those parts of our lives were stuck. Going on the camino, putting ourselves in a completely new environment, having the time to reflect, meeting people from all parts of the world, and taking advantage of the amazing freedom the journey offered helped move us forward to where we are today. This journey was life changing in many ways. We met and connected with people from different parts of the world and, regardless of background, found everyone to be so similar. Many people on the camino are undergoing some kind of transition during which they are evaluating their lives, choices, and values, and many are wondering excitedly how they will move forward with their lives. Our own transformational journeys inspired us to share our findings and to help others.

In this book we offer unique and varied perspectives on the feeling of being stuck and getting unstuck. Despite the fact that we are from different parts of the world (Terry from California and Nina from Sweden), from different industries, and from very different kinds of lives, there we were, walking the camino at the same time and looking for similar insights. We came to learn that getting stuck is a universal issue that can affect anyone, regardless of someone's background. We also found that most people want and need tools to assist them in becoming unstuck. This set us on a path to learn more about getting unstuck. The book you are reading distills our hours of research, countless conversations with others, and analyses of our own experiences.

The camino is marked with a series of yellow arrows that lets pilgrims know that they are headed in the right direction and moving toward their goal. While walking on this path it's a relief to learn that you are just where you need to be. You may not be able to see the end of the path, but you feel assured that you are on your way. Having a yellow arrow to follow was a simple yet powerful experience for us! Upon completion of the camino, we missed that clear sign that we were headed in the right direction, and we wanted to learn how we might come to detect the yellow arrows in our lives. After all, when you're stuck in your life, it's a relief to be able to focus on the next step and know that you are on the right track. And just like on the camino, if you can't find your yellow arrow, you need to stop, think, and regroup. This book will give you the tools to find and follow your own arrows in life.

So where are the arrows in your life? Are you where you want to be and headed in the direction you want to go in? Or do you feel uneasy, dissatisfied, or unsure of how to change your situation? We know so many people, including ourselves, who could have used a book like this when feeling stuck. We hope it gives you the tools to deal with the challenges and changes in your life.

You are welcome to read this book in the order presented, or you can focus on the tools you think will serve you best. You might find that some of the tools seem contradictory. For example, one tool focuses on how important it is to just take a first step when making a decision without worrying too much about the overall situation. Another tool is all about allowing yourself time and creating the space for your next step. This is because we know that each situation looks different from person to person and requires different solutions based on one's stage in life.

We believe that love relationships are the most significant aspects of our lives. In our discussions with people we have met, when love relationships were lost or changed, the loss was often deep and devastating. Therefore, we have dedicated one chapter to becoming unstuck in the situation of lost or changed love relationships, and we discuss the best tools for each situation.

Life is so fulfilling when we are able to enjoy each day. Being unstuck allows us to do just that — enjoy each day! Whatever happens, if you utilize these powerful tools, you will be able to assess the situation, decide the next steps, and take action. We wrote this book to help you create a life that has more meaning and gives you more happiness!

Chapter 1

Managing Life Transitions

I do not recognize myself anymore, and I feel that I am going nowhere. I know I want something more in life, but feel I will hurt people that I really love if I make the necessary changes.

Transitions are a natural part of our lives. We finish our schooling, begin a career, find a partner, change jobs, change relationships, dispute old facts, and evolve some of our beliefs and traditions. Most transitions will go smoothly, and perhaps we won't even recognize that we are or just were in a transition. But then suddenly one day we feel stuck. Maybe you realize you do not have the education you need, lose someone you loved, get fired from a job, have an unfulfilling relationship, or somehow just lose your direction in life. This can happen at any stage of life, young or old.

When we reflect upon our own lives, it becomes clear that how we manage major changes is based on our perception of the situation and whether we have the insight and courage to address that situation. Being stuck can happen when we persist in doing something the same way, each time thinking it will give us a different result. Or maybe we know we have a problem, but we are not ready to come face-to-face with it. Or we might know that something is wrong and we don't like the way it feels, but our fear of the unknown is such that we just stay put.

Becoming aware of a situation and then deciding to do something to change it are vital first steps. Developing our own intentions — or our own yellow arrows — gives us a way to adapt to major changes. However, most of us have not developed a life intention, action steps, or clear arrows. So, when something changes and we need to adapt, we may not have a clear method for doing so. Therefore, we might resist the change since we may not like it or we fear what is happening. We might become unmotivated, feel unhappy, or feel like a victim in a situation, with limited understanding of how to take positive action.

This contributes to a feeling of being "stuck in a rut" or "frozen in place." What does that look like? Words that come to mind include "immobile," "locked in," "at a loss," "stalled," and "at a standstill." An antonym for stuck is "free." What else does stuck look like? It can include feeling a lack of excitement or feeling bored, drained, or trapped.

People who are stuck might describe their situation in the following ways. Can you relate to any of them?

» *I cannot get over being left by my partner. I feel like I lost my past, my future, and definitely myself.*

» *I do not like my job anymore. It takes a lot of energy, and my family complains about me always being so negative and easily irritated. The thought of starting to deal with my work situation makes me feel scared. I have no idea where and how to start.*

» *My partner is pushing me for marriage. I am unsure about my feelings for him and if he is the right one for me. However, I have invested so much in our relationship, and I am also afraid of never finding a new partner. Maybe marrying him will make us more compatible and stronger as a couple.*

» *My life is not what I thought it would be, both when I think of my job and my relationship with my children. Because of this my health is deteriorating. I have become overweight and am tired all the time. I want to change my life but I do not know where to begin!*

» *My spouse is dominating and non-communicative. We are not meant to be together, but I hate the thought of divorce. I know counseling won't work for us. I feel I have no options here. I'm so unhappy!*

» *I am so very lonely. I am afraid to let people know the real me, since I don't feel that I am a lovable or even likeable person. All I do at home is watch TV. I feel stuck and want to change, but don't know how to do so.*

I, Terry, want to share a time when things were not right in my life, but I had a hard time recognizing what was happening. Overall, I have been very fortunate with success in career, great family and friends, and many wonderful experiences. However, I have been hesitant to listen to my inner voice, my intuition, when it comes to deep relationships. You will learn more about why in a later story. But, I want to share this story now.

A few years ago I had an important breakfast meeting with a major benefactor and friend. I had been looking forward to our time together from both a friendship and business standpoint. Shortly into the breakfast, he asked me why I was eating my porridge with a fork. I looked down and saw, to my amazement, that truly I had picked up a fork instead of a spoon and hadn't even noticed the difference. However, in trying to cover this up, I indicated that I always eat my porridge with my fork. After a less productive meeting than usual, we stopped at my car to say farewell, and then we both noticed it. The left side of my car was so damaged that the car door on the driver's side could not be opened! I started sweating and feeling so embarrassed when I suddenly recalled my scraping against a steel pole when coming into the parking area and that I had needed to climb out the passenger side to go into the meeting.

After saying goodbye and leaving the area, I almost immediately received a call from my doctor, who asked me to come to his office right away. My friend had called my doctor, who is a good friend to both of us. What a gift! At the doctor's office, it was clear that I was physically fine, but emotionally and mentally I was at a very low point. That was a turning point in my life. How could I have gotten to a situation where I could be acting in such a bizarre manner? What was going on in my life that caused this mishap and several other issues that were atypical of my behavior? I realized that day that I had been subconsciously stuck in dealing with a deep relationship, and only now was I willing to bring it to a conscious part of my thinking. At that moment, I knew what had me immobilized in a key area of my life. This is when I promised myself that I would start to take immediate action to become unstuck.

So, I, Terry was in this unhappy place, and for a long time, I didn't realize it. You might be in that kind of place too. But rather than waiting for somebody from the outside to take action, wouldn't it be better if you were able recognize the situation on your own and do something about it right now? In the next chapter, we will address how to become more aware of your situation. The great news is that when we begin to recognize our circumstances, we have the outstanding opportunity to begin the process of getting unstuck. We might say, *"Ok, I know why I am at this spot. It scares me to know this and it feels even scarier to take action to change the situation. But, I will begin!"* By facing our situation and our fears consciously, we can take action to get back on track and achieve personal growth.

Next, we will turn our attention to why we get stuck, and then we will discuss the actions and the tools one can utilize to successfully transition to a new life situation.

Chapter 2

Frozen in Place. Why?

Getting or being stuck may be related to your relationships, your work situation, your health, or other situations that are hurting your state of well-being. Terry's experience underscores how unaware we can be of our situations, but it also shows how hard it can be to determine why this is happening. After all, he was a successful and respected CEO, but he didn't recognize what was occurring in his life that caused this mishap. How could something like this happen? We will now address some of the most common reasons why we may not be aware, motivated, or able to transition from a difficult life situation. No one would intentionally want to be stuck or frozen in place, so why would this happen? What is it that gets us to a position where we are almost immobilized?

Not admitting to ourselves

Oftentimes, we think a negative issue is so small that it could not really affect our quality of life. Ah, but what is small to your conscious mind can be a huge issue to your subconscious mind. PhD Catherine Collautt states, "Scientists will tell you that the power of the subconscious is perhaps a million times greater than that of the conscious mind!"[1] Because of the great power of the subconscious mind it is important for us to "establish healthy and functional rapport between our conscious goals, efforts, and desires and the powerhouse that is our subconscious mind."[2]

Many of us also have a hard time admitting to ourselves that we are unable to deal with a negative situation and that we don't know how to transition out of it. It may be difficult to admit that the choices you have made or neglected to make have taken you to a place that no longer works for you. We find it easier to avoid dealing with the behaviors or situations that are negatively affecting our state of mind. We might distract ourselves from our feelings of stress, hurt, boredom, or lack of motivation. We get stuck because we are not aware of ourselves in the present moment. Instead, we focus on the past or the future, withdrawing into our minds rather than connecting ourselves to the here and now. By this, we avoid the insights of the now, whether consciously or subconsciously. The present moment is, however, where we need to be so that we can hear our inner voice and guidance and as Eckhart Tolle, one of the most spiritually influential persons in the

---

1   Found in the pdf "Success V Freedom" on catherinecollautt.com/subscriber-downloads/success-vs-freedom

2   The five step guide to reprogramming your subconscious mind can be found here: catherinecollautt.com/subscriber-downloads/success-vs-freedom

world, says, "Realize deeply that the present moment is all you ever have."

Fear of admitting to others

Sometimes it's hard admitting to yourself you are stuck, and admitting that to others might be even harder. You might have been doing great in all areas of your life, and it may be difficult to confide in others, like friends, family, and colleagues that you feel you have failed in something, whether it be marriage, career, finances, or decisions you have made that you now regret. This may be especially true if people around you questioned your decisions, making it even harder to admit that your choices did not in fact work out.

Fear of changing your situation

Even if you are fully aware of your situation, you might be stuck because you are afraid of the consequences of changing your situation. Often, we have to give up something important to change our situation or reach the next level. You might face financial consequences, like giving up the big wonderful home you love or drastically changing your lifestyle. It could mean letting go of the security of your marriage or of your workplace. You might worry about how your children will cope with a change or how they will react to you. You might also be afraid of being unpopular or of disappointing people around you, like your parents, your spouse, or your friends.

No clear intentions for your life

The voice of the status quo is so strong in all of our lives. Could the future be worse than the present if we make a change? At least with the status quo, we know what will happen and, therefore, don't have to speculate on "what if." We might convince ourselves that a change may be significantly more negative, so we stay where we are even if we suffer. Not having a plan or an intention for your life in six months, in a year, or in several years' time can also keep you frozen or unmotivated to change. As Carl Jung, the Swiss psychotherapist and psychiatrist and one of the most important people in the history of psychology, says: "Your vision will become clear when you can look into your own heart. Who looks outside dreams; who looks inside, awakes." While dreaming about what we desire is good, translating these dreams into action steps is most important.

You don't have tools to use

Maybe now you more clearly see why you are stuck, but you still don't know how to change your situation. Perhaps you have never felt stuck before, or maybe the tools you previously used to change your situation are no longer working. So, how shall you go about the change? In this book, you will learn about proven tools that you can use to become unstuck. You will gain a toolbox of possible approaches and strategies, depending on your specific situation and your personality.

Each of the tools provides a way for change and can help you create your own yellow arrows, which will take you where you want to go in your life.

Chapter 3

10 Tools of Wisdom

Now you have a basic understanding of what being stuck means and why people get stuck. Based on countless discussions, extensive research, and counseling friends and acquaintances, we have identified the most effective tools that give you the power to change your state of mind and your situation. Depending on your situation and your personality, you will find that some tools are more relevant than others. You might benefit from all of the tools or maybe just of a few of them. You might use the tools following a particular sequence, while another person might use them in a different order.

The toolbox consists of 10 different tools. Our rationale behind the sequence of the tools is the following: Tools 1and 2 are about you and your mindset. The next ones, tools 3 and 4, are about taking action. We then examine tools 5 through 8, which help you understand and deal with issues that keep you stuck. The last tools, 8 through 10, are all about how to find your passion, what you want in life, and the different resources available to you besides these tools.

These tools can be used to help you get out of any stuck situation or life experience. However, in our research, we heard time and again that love relationships are the most frequent and challenging way that people become stuck. So, in Chapter 4, following our discussion of all of the tools, we dive deeper into romantic love. Here we share a few stories from people who experienced lost love and how they finally moved past their painful situations. As part of each of the four stories, we share the tools they used to find their yellow arrows, to be able to move on and get a new direction in their lives.

The last chapter, Chapter 5, helps you gain insight into what tools and what sequence are right for you. This chapter is a very important part of the work you will do to get unstuck, since it will help you see clearly what to do next. Have a look at Chapter 5 now so that you can understand its format. This will help prepare you to think more deeply and specifically about the different tools. In addition, we have placed questions after each tool that will help you in your next steps. This is so you can start building your toolbox right away. The questions are marked with: ➡️

Let's now move into the tools that will help you with your arrows of direction in life!

Tool 1: Be Kind to Yourself

Are you aware of the voice in your head? You might not be fully aware of this voice, but it's constantly talking to you. Your inner voice can be a great friend, but many times it's also your worst critic. When you start listening to what you tell yourself, you can start understanding if your inner voice is a kind and supporting voice or if it's the opposite. Maybe it's your inner voice that actually turns out to be your worst enemy. Not others and not the outside world, but your own inner voice. In *The Untethered Soul*, Michael A. Singer says: "Only you can take inner freedom away from yourself, or give it to yourself. Nobody else can." When you become conscious of the fact that the voice in your head is not you but that you are the one who hears it, you can start working with it. Understanding this, you will have the profound opportunity to decide if you want to listen to that voice. Even better, you can change the way your inner voice works, so it becomes kind and supportive.

"When examining 400 scientific papers 2015, psychology professor Mark Leary" concluded that nothing was more important than how we talk to ourselves. He showed, "There is no other single factor that has such a strong connection to emotional well-being than self-acceptance. To be able to make friends with yourself and having a kind and understanding attitude towards your (perceived) flaws and shortcomings, is thus something important and meaningful."[3]

Your inner voice

What do you say to yourself? How would you describe your inner voice? And how does that voice actually affect you? I, Terry, for a very long time did not identify the impact of my inner voice. I just never gave it much thought. But when I started to listen and understand what I was doing to myself, I was able to make one of the biggest changes in my life. Here is my story.

As the youngest child in a family of four children, I felt that I was not unique or special to my parents. Getting their attention seemed to be difficult for me no matter how hard I tried. Therefore, I developed two personal traits. First, I had to be perfect in anything I would try or else not do it. The second was to do all I could to please my parents both in action and in words. I continually told myself that I didn't measure up. Therefore, I was insecure and lacked confidence, even at a very young age. That feeling continued in me as I matured, to the point that I felt I was not sufficient enough to be loved or accepted just for being me.

In reality, I had been blessed with great physical, social, and intellectual skills. I was very good in sports, good in school, popular

---

3   Agneta Lagercrants quotes Mark Leary in her post "Self-Compassion – What does it mean?" on her webpage <u>agnetalagercrantz.se/</u> <u>self-compassion-what-does-it-mean/</u>

among friends, and always focused on achievement. Life worked at that level, even though I didn't feel that I measured up to others' expectations. When getting into the competitive environment of college and career, my inner voice continued to push me into thinking I was not sufficient, creating a continued lack of confidence and insecurity that kept me from trying new activities and pursuing new interests.

I have one very graphic example of this. I went to my university partly because I wanted to play basketball. My first year, I played basketball and was a starter. However, as I looked at the following year, I was certain I would not start, but would be a high-ranking substitute. What did I do about this? I chose not to join the team my sophomore year. My inner voice said, "If I cannot start, then I am not achieving what I should." So I didn't even try! As I look back at this and other opportunities I missed, it makes me sad. I now know that it was my critical inner voice that prevented me from even trying. Thankfully, despite this, I was able to move into a fulfilling career after college and enjoy external success in the healthcare field.

There were great times and even years, but underneath it all, I felt I did not measure up. I continued to feel insecure and needed constant reassurance. Although I sincerely loved my work, I did not feel complete. The same applied to my personal relationships: I just didn't feel like I measured up. My negative inner voice had the strongest grip on me, but I wasn't aware of it.

Finally, after years of not feeling in balance or being content with who I was, I had an eye-opening experience. A close friend was going through a major transition, both in career and love relationship. He asked me for some advice, which I readily provided. When I had finished, my friend was very grateful, but said: "Terry, why haven't you done what you are suggesting to me? Your advice is so insightful, and I wonder if it is not about time for you to start applying it to your own life?" Oh my! This set me to several sleepless nights! I valued my friend's input tremendously and didn't realize how I came across to people who knew me well. The people who were closest to me could see that I was struggling and that my outer and inner worlds were not at all in sync.

I started to understand the impact my inner voice was having on my life and my relationships, and I started to truly listen to myself. Through self-analysis, friends, coaching, and readings, I connected the damage I inflicted upon myself with my critical inner voice. I realized that I could change my world "just" by changing how I spoke to myself. I understood that no matter how successful I was, it was my inner world that made all the difference! I also understood that feelings like contentment, balance, and happiness come from within. Once I understood and accepted this, I was able to transition from a person who was dependent on the opinion of others to a person who is at peace with who I am and who can live an adventurous yet harmonic life.

While I am so fortunate for my awakening, it's sad to think back on those years of insecurity when I was the one who hindered myself living to my fullest. Deep inside, I did not feel enough. I thought I needed to be the greatest in everything to be loved and to be worthy of the opportunities I pursued. So many capable, successful, and respected people have admitted that this is one of their biggest issues, something that hinders them from being in full balance, from feeling in peace with themselves and their lives. I know that there are many out there feeling and experiencing the same as I did. I hope that through my story, you will be able to see that it's you and no one else who has the key to your greatness, inner peace, and happiness. So, use your key, open up to the deepened understanding of yourself, and never ever give your key away!

The world outside you

We have been discussing feelings that are brought on by your unkind inner voice, but that voice can also be fed by outside factors. For example, you might compare yourself to others and begin to think that you do not deserve the life you have or that you have not achieved enough in your life. People around you seem to have so much more than you have. Perhaps they enjoy successful careers, have created a lovely family, and go on amazing vacations. They seem to live a fantastic life. Comparing yourself to others can seriously damage your feelings of self-worth. Why do it? We don't know what issues, insecurities, or challenges might hide behind what we see. Very often we just see the "tip of the iceberg," but have no clue what is underneath, what the other person really thinks or feels.

Another possible negative outside influence is that we act based on what we believe other people might think and expect from us. We can choose to consider other people and their opinions, but we do not need to let them steer our lives. We need to realize that everyone's journey is different. It's liberating to come to peace with the thought that I have my own unique contribution and that I do not need to worry about where others are in their lives or what they think. We need to focus on our own lives and trust our own path, having faith that we are where we should be. Let's become still enough to hear what greater possibilities life has in mind for us and not live someone else's version of it.

What can we do to help us stay kind and positive toward ourselves when our critical voice kicks in? We want to share what we do when the limiting, critical inner voice is getting too loud.

Your own mantra

The first action relates to your inner voice, the voice that gives you negative thoughts about yourself and your situation. When your critical inner voice appears, stop and take some deep breaths. Focus on your breath and then quietly say some powerful, comforting words, a short mantra like "I am enough. I am exactly where I should be," or "I am enough. All is well." It's important to stop, breathe, and quickly and decisively replace your negative inner chatter with your own mantra. In other words, use your mantra to get your inner voice to work for you. In the beginning, it might feel odd, but after practicing this simple step awhile, you will be amazed at the difference it makes. So next time negative or diminishing thoughts about yourself occur, breathe and switch to the mantra that will help you refocus and bring you to a better and calmer state of mind.

Blossom at every stage of life

The second action relates to comparing yourself to others or feeling that you aren't where you should be. This is about adopting the belief that you can blossom at every stage in life. It will give you assurance that you have plenty of time and opportunities in your life ahead, so why feel too old, behind, or unsettled with yourself? When that feeling appears, we suggest you view your life in its whole, a life that blossoms over and over again! This takes the pressure off of having to achieve everything now or in a certain order. It also gives you the necessary peace of mind to make good decisions about your path. Consider every day an opportunity to blossom. This attitude will help as you try new things or change a situation that did not work out as you had planned.

I, Terry, left my full-time job eighteen months ago. I loved my job as CEO of a major university hospital and health system, but I wanted more balance in my life. During my long career, and particularly my last ten years, I had achieved all I wanted, and after six years in my position, I decided it was time to leave full-time work. I have always been adventurous, and for over fifteen years I'd had a dream of going on the camino. So, as part of my transition, I decided to do just that. My life until then had been mostly focused around my work, but now I wanted to have a true break from my everyday life, to reorient myself, to reinvent myself, and to blossom again! I wanted to experience life in new ways! So, I packed my bag and went on the camino.

Little did I know then how much the camino would impact my life and how much I would grow by doing this long walk in a foreign country. I did not know anybody when I arrived and had no idea how the trip would unfold. It was incredible how much I learned about so many new things in life, about other people, and, foremost, about myself. This journey truly helped me shift to a more balanced and joyful life where today I again do what I love to do. I continue to work in an industry I'm passionate about, but I also have the flexibility to continue exploring the world as well as being with my beloved ones. My life has blossomed again as I learn new things, develop personally, meet new people, and enjoy new experiences. I am full of excitement for each new day!

It's sad when we think we are behind. This has nothing to do with age. You can have the same feeling when you are 21, 43, 50, or 65. If you have the feeling that you have not achieved as much as the people around you, whether it be your friends or your colleagues, we implore you to follow the motto: blossom at any stage in life! You can and will blossom over and over again! This truly allows you a lot of time to reach all the things you wanted, but maybe in another order and pace than others might have experienced. When you relieve yourself from the pressure of having to achieve things in a specific order and at a certain age, you will begin to enjoy your life so much more. You might even find that all the goals that were important to you are accomplished one by one, and those that were not as important disappear.

Here some tips and questions that can help quiet a critical inner voice:

1. Practice positive self-talk. Don't say anything to yourself that you wouldn't say to a friend. Be gentle and encouraging with yourself. If a thought that does not serve you enters your mind, just let it pass and focus on positive words, like your own mantra and self-talk.

2. Remember you are not alone and that everybody has ups and downs! This is life! It's easy to start making changes too quickly and to go looking for big-picture solutions when you just had one bad day. Don't do it. The calmer and more in sync with yourself you are, the better the quality of your decisions and direction.

3. When you feel stuck, how do you feel about it? Is it totally negative? Our experience is that being stuck can produce something very positive. You might say: "What, positive being stuck!? No way!" But the feeling of being stuck also gives you an opportunity to reflect, to take a break in your routine, and to think about what you want. What are the benefits of change? What are the positives of being stuck? Can you think of being stuck as an opportunity to develop and grow?

4. Are you comfortable with failure? Many times when something or someone fails, it depends on a lot of pieces that move around, things out of our control. Remember that it's not necessarily about you! What if we could look at failure as a natural part of life and as

a chance to take a step back and reflect on the current situation? In other words, what happens to you is one thing, but how you perceive it and how it affects your life is another.

5. Review the expectations you set on yourself. Are they your own expectations? Or are they expectations from somebody else or expectations you think somebody else has on you? First, sort that out. If your feelings relate to others' expectations, go back and read the section "The World Outside You" again. If these are your own expectations, do you fully embrace the fact that being good at everything is not possible? We all have only a set amount of time, and you need to decide what you want and what you do not want to spend time on. Make a conscious choice, and you will soon see that where you invest your energy, you will start getting the results you want. Again, remember to check what you are telling yourself! Is your inner voice a supporting voice or a critical voice?

 Question to you:

In chapter 5, you will start creating your toolbox. Could this tool be one of the tools in your toolbox for change?

Tool 2: Mindset

"Life is only as good as your mindset"

Why does life seem to go easily — almost effortlessly — for some people, whereas for other people it seems to be a struggle? No doubt every person's life looks different. In every life there are ups and downs, but some people seem to have a stronger and longer positive flow in life than others. Why is that? Is it based on what happens to you externally, or is it based on the internal translation of what happens? How we perceive a situation is based on our own thoughts and goes far beyond the external circumstances. We cannot control external events, people, or many situations, but we can control how we view and act upon them.

Much of what modern psychology knows about our mindset and our belief system comes from the work of Stanford University professor, Carol Dweck, described in her book *Mindset: The New Psychology of Success*. Dweck found that one of the most basic beliefs we carry about ourselves has to do with how we view and inhabit our personalities. Dweck divides the beliefs into a "fixed mindset" and a "growth mindset." The fixed mindset assumes that our character, intelligence, and creative ability are givens that we cannot change in a meaningful way. The growth mindset on the other hand believes one can acquire any given ability if one invests in it. In her research Dweck found that a growth mindset creates a passion for learning rather than a hunger for approval.

Dweck writes, "As you begin to understand the fixed and growth mindsets, you will see exactly how one thing leads to another — how a belief that your qualities are carved in stone leads to a host of thoughts and actions, and how a belief that your qualities can be cultivated leads to a host of different thoughts and actions, taking you down an entirely different road."[4]

I, Nina, have always had a mindset thinking that things are possible, that I can achieve or get what I want as long as I know what I want. When I was around ten years old, horses became a great interest of mine. I started riding once a week, and soon horses were all I could talk about.

There was one public stable in my town, and my biggest wish was to become a groom and have my own horse to take care of. I fell deeply in love with Ariel, a stubborn and very unique fjord horse. I had made up my mind, I would become a groom of Ariel. At the beginning I could not become the number one or the number two groom. Instead I had to aim for the number three groom, lowest in the hierarchy. At least now I could be in charge when the other grooms did not want or could not do some of the tasks needed. My journey to become a groom started by hanging around as much as possible in the stable, doing non-horse related tasks, like carrying out water to the horses, sweeping the stable floor, and sometimes if lucky bringing Ariel to the pasture. After months and months of

---

4   www.brainpickings.org/2014/01/29/carol-dweck-mindset/

slowly but surely working myself into the system, I finally became a groom of Ariel. Jippi!

My years in the stable were very rewarding, from having to show up day after day, not knowing if I would get to touch a horse, to my biggest dream ultimately coming true — becoming the number one groom of Ariel! And this was only one aspect of the reward. The additional reward for my persistence was the great camaraderie that resulted in many of the "stable girls" becoming and still being my closest friends.

My experience at the stable was a great early life lesson in mindset. It is a lesson that I have benefitted from in many situations, like establishing myself in a new country, getting a job, going on a long journey like the camino, and encouraging and coaching others. My daughter brought this up in a speech she gave to me when I turned 50. She stated that I taught her and her brother to have a positive mindset and encouraged them to dare to go for what they want and to not give in!

In the last chapter we focused on self-talk, which is also part of mindset. That chapter focused on a more internal perspective, whereas in this chapter we focus on a more external view, how you think and go about things. Your belief in your ability to succeed sets the stage for how you think, behave, and feel. So, it's much more important what you think about yourself and your capabilities, your situation, and your future than where you actually are right now. The quote from Henry Ford, founder of the Ford Motor Company and origin of many insightful quotes about business, leadership, and life, is for us a great inspiration:

"Whether you think you can, or you think you can't — you're right."

What we tell ourselves and what we believe significantly affect our lives. Are your beliefs supporting beliefs, or are they limiting beliefs? Usually, it's very easy to hear your limiting beliefs. You might have your goal or even your purpose sorted out, but your beliefs can stop you. They may tell you: "I do not know enough," "I am too old," or "The time is not right." Those kinds of limiting beliefs stop you from pursuing your next step. But supporting beliefs, like "I can do this" or "If it does not work, I will do something else," allow you to keep moving forward, expanding, and doing something different. It's also important to be aware of what words you use. Do you use words that come from a powerful place within you, like: "I am…" or "I have…"? Or do you use words from a weaker place: "I will try," "I think I can," and "Maybe I am able…"? Remember, what you believe is what you bring about, and this is why you need to become aware of what you are telling yourself.

Why is it so important to be aware of your thoughts when you are in a frozen situation? In the TEDx Talk "Getting stuck in the negatives and how to get unstuck," Alison Ledgerwood, PhD in Social Psychology, talks about how much easier it is to get stuck in negative thoughts than in positive ones. This means we need to work harder to see the upside of things.[5] For example, think of a situation when you gave a presentation that you thought went very well. After the presentation, even if the majority of the audience gave you positive feedback, what you will likely remember is the one negative or challenging comment. Why does this happen? For most people the criticizing voice seems to be more dominant. Although we shouldn't ignore helpful critique, we should focus on the positives at least as much as we do on the negatives. Thinking positively takes discipline.

So, the question is, can you change your mindset? The powerful answer is yes! Yes, you can! Remember: you own your thoughts. They do not own you! The better questions are: Do you want to change you mindset? Do you want your mindset to be a supporting or a limiting factor in your life? Will you consciously work to change your mindset so it serves you better? How can you think in new ways? How can you create some new habits that support you in where you want to move?

What can you do to change your mindset?

Focus on strengths

Companies have identified the value of gathering and sharing success stories as a tool for growth and positive momentum.

---

5   www.youtube.com/watch?v=qbXtaIYRICE

Individuals can also benefit from this. We can develop our own success stories that remind, inspire, and encourage us when we doubt our own abilities. We all have stories to tell about achievements we have obtained, times when we were able to drive through, and times when we succeeded in what we wanted even if it was not easy. So remember your strengths and build your own success stories that help you with your mindset and achieving what you want.

Focus on a growth mindset

When you have a growth mindset, you look at your abilities and talents as something that can be developed over time. Professor Carol Dweck showed that when students were taught the growth mindset, they understood that every time they were pushed out of their comfort zones to learn something new and difficult, the neurons in their brains would form new, stronger connections, and over time they would get smarter.[6]

Focus on gratitude

An easy yet powerful way to impact your mindset is to regularly write down things you are grateful for. Research out of UC Davis shows that writing just a few minutes a day about things you are grateful for can dramatically boost your happiness, well-being, and even your health.

---

6   www.ted.com/talks/carol_dweck_the_power_of_believing_that_you_can_improve

"Gratitude journals and other gratitude practices often seem so simple and basic; in our studies, we often have people keep gratitude journals for just three weeks. And yet the results have been overwhelming. We've studied more than one thousand people, from ages eight to 80, and found that people who practice gratitude consistently report a host of benefits,"[7] says Robert Emmons, the world's leading scientific expert on gratitude.

The writing can be as simple as "I am grateful for the sunny morning," or "I am grateful for my friend coming to visit tonight." Just insert anything you are grateful for: "I am grateful for..." This writing helps you focus and be aware of how many things in your life there are to be grateful for. The more you focus on what is good in your life, the more you will grow the parts that you are grateful for, and it will also allow you to feel more joy, balance, and inspiration.

There are different theories on how often and what to write in your gratitude journal. Both of us are writing gratitude journals, focusing on three to five new things each time that we are grateful for. This works the best for us since it truly shows how much there is to be thankful for, and it's also a good history line one can go back to and be inspired by when having a low day. So try out writing a gratitude journal and find out what suits you the best. We strongly believe it helps you build a more positive mindset.

---

7   greatergood.berkeley.edu/article/item/why_gratitude_is_good/

Repeat good news

Another way to change our mindset is to repeat good news and share it with others. It's easy to get absorbed talking about negative things happening to us, but when you start focusing on the good things instead, your energy and mindset will change. Soon you will realize your day or situation was not as bad as at first sight.

Change perspective

It also makes sense to look at things from another or even completely opposite perspective. The same facts can have different meanings when seen from different perspectives. In order to challenge your assumptions and thoughts about something, you can ask: "What if I view my situation or challenge from an opposite perspective?" or "How can the perceived negative experience or situation open new possibilities?" These questions come from a positive, open place instead of a limiting, negative place.

Questions you can ask to change your mindset:

1. How could you shift mindset? Choose one way discussed above and begin using it right now.

2. You can easily start changing your mindset by focusing on what is already good in your life, so why not start writing down what you are grateful for today?

3. Can you notice the difference in your thinking and behavior when you actively focus on changing your mindset to something positive? You can do this by asking, *"What am I feeling great about right now?"* This question will help you to look for reasons to feel great, instead of the opposite.

4. How much do you think a change in your mindset would help you move away from a negative situation to something new?

5. Can you look at things in a new way? Perhaps you could view pressure as an opportunity to achieve or an opportunity for growth.

 Question to you:

In Chapter 5 you will start creating your toolbox. Could this tool be one of the tools in your toolbox for change?

_____

Tool 3: Make a Decision to Take a First Step!

"If you're waiting for a sign, THIS is it!"

You may have a feeling you are not happy, motivated, or content with your current situation. You might fully perceive what is wrong and what needs to be done to change your current dynamics. Our focus here is on those who know that their current life is not fulfilling and who are very discontent for some reason. Many of us tend to "put our heads in the sand" and not deal with what is making us unhappy or dissatisfied. Instead, we find different ways to distract ourselves from having to truly face our issue. These distractions, unfortunately, are mostly only temporary and add to our problems. At some point, we must begin to face the fact that something must change. But what, when, and how? We both have had situations where we forced ourselves out of a negative situation to get ourselves to a better place. Making a decision to take that first step, as difficult as that might be, has been the way to get positive movement and have other good things follow. Getting some positive momentum is critical!

Our friend Jenni from Canada, whom we met on the camino, needed to take a first step to get out of her frozen situation.

"I knew for about three years that I was not on the right life path, and I was not living the fulfilled life I truly wanted. The problem was that even though I somehow felt something was wrong, I knew I was very fortunate. I had a great job, great home, great

vacations, lived in a great city, and had great friends. That allowed me to coast for years, but while doing that the feeling of unhappiness inside grew stronger. I finally realized my life had to change and I needed to develop a plan for that.

The next challenge for me was that I started by trying to develop the perfect plan. Being a perfectionist I felt I needed to figure everything out at once: my ideal new place, my ideal new job and my ideal lifestyle. Yes, I had a long list of things I needed to figure out. Adding to that I was also suffering from analysis paralysis. I read every book possible, did all the personality tests and lamented during months of conversations. For sure I did learn a lot about myself and gained new insights that have been very valuable. But, I was all talk, no action!"

So Jenni felt completely overwhelmed when thinking of her overall situation and about her future. She felt stuck, almost paralyzed, in her life. During this time a friend happened to mention a possible avenue for her to consider. It was the Camino de Santiago, the 500 mile walk in northern Spain. Jenni got inspired about what her friend told her and started reading and learning about the camino. She decided to go!

Making that decision to go on the camino gave her new energy, so she started to prepare for the walk. Jenni's first big step was to ask for seven weeks of vacation. As you can imagine, that was not an easy task given her demanding job. While waiting for her manager's slow response, she grew restless. The day she was called to the manager to get his feedback on her vacation request, she instead *handed in her resignation! Having been stuck in her situation for so long, she suddenly had the energy to start dealing with the different parts of her life that were not fulfilling anymore. So Jenni resigned from her job. Building on this momentum, she also decided to sell her house so that she could begin the process of developing her new life intention without being tied to any location. What happened inside Jenni that made her finally make the big and bold decision to take these steps?*

"The big shift in my thinking came with the realization that I could start by simply not doing all of the things that I knew were wrong. Having felt stuck and unfulfilled for such a long time, I now made a commitment to myself to let my soul and intuition guide me. What I truly felt I needed most deeply was to be outside, moving with momentum and meeting as many new perspectives as possible.

The other thing that helped me come to this big decision was the knowledge that by only asking for vacation to do the camino, and not quitting full-stop, I was really letting myself down. The feeling of letting myself down felt like rotting a hole through my belly! I was ashamed of and deeply disappointed by that, so I made a promise to myself to not let myself down any longer! Thankfully I had a strong and supportive friend and family network who I could discuss this with, and every single one of them said 'Wow!' and 'Go for it, I've got your back and will support you." I would have done it anyway, but having that support really helped unleash my confidence!"

The Jenni who eight months later put on her backpack to start her camino was a Jenni who basically only owned what she was carrying in the pack. Yes, only the pack on her back, but now she felt in charge of her future for the first time in years and was full of excitement for her new, free life.

Looking back on this time where Jenni finally made the decision that she no longer could stay in the unfulfilled life situation, Jenni now realizes how right the decision to make that first step was. It was a decision full of doubt and insecurity about her path forward, but even more a decision for her new life. "The camino was truly the first step on my path! I also committed to focusing on the present and not yet making future plans. I decided to trust that I would know my next steps and that they would come to me at the right time. So my first step was needing to be outside and moving. During one steep uphill climb on the camino I suddenly realized that I needed to be with family! As my next step after the camino, I went to Zimbabwe where I spent invaluable family time with my sister and her family. What happened during that time was amazing! One day I met a longtime neighbor of my sister. He is a modern day explorer and the connection with him was immediate. I have truly fallen in love for the first time and we already talk about our future together. It's truly amazing, because what I've been most frightened of my whole life is the thing I want most for my life now! For you who read this, I hope I can encourage you to make the decision to take that first step on your way to more fulfillment and to the happiness that I am enjoying now."

Photo by Jenni M

Ok, so that is a great story, but it is Jenni's story. So you ask, *"What about me?"* You might not want to totally change your life as she did. You might not be able to afford to make big changes to your life, due to financial, time, or relationship constraints. You might just have a feeling that you could be and do so much more, but you don't know where to start. Finally, you might ask, when is the right time to start? These common questions reveal some of the biggest reasons we continue being stuck in a situation we want to change.

You decide when the time is right

The fact is that you can wait forever for the right timing. You are the only one who can decide when the time is right.

You will never be able to have the full picture, no matter if it is about a relationship, some important work, or about your overall situation. This is when you just need to make the decision to take the first step, as difficult as it might seem. Don't wait for the approval of others. Two simple yet powerful questions that have helped us many times are: *"If not now, then when?"* and *"If not I, then who?"* When you stand in the middle of the parts in your life you want to change, and you don't know when and how, the answer is: *"Make a decision to take a first step now and things will start happening!"* Positive change begins this way! With the first step you now have power over yourself.

It can be so hard to take the first step when the rest of the journey is unclear or maybe even completely unknown. But if you take the first step, you gain momentum and are much more likely to take the next step. When you have taken that first critical step, you have already done the hardest part. Congratulations! Now you have movement. After this, the next step will come so much more easily. You will mentally move from resistance, doubt, or fear to *"Yes, I am doing this. Yes, I can and I will!"* Many times one can get frozen and even move backwards when looking too far into the future. If too ambitious, then any task or change can seem nearly impossible. Acknowledge what pace is good for you. Will it help you to focus on the big picture or to take things in steps? Sometimes it helps to shift your focus away from the distant future to the present moment. Then you can focus on taking one step at a time. So take a small step today and continue doing it. You can then reach your goal at a pace that is right for you.

Making a decision is certainly a way to move forward, though it can also lead to failure, rejection, or mistakes. There is always a risk for that. But if you take no action, then it is most likely that nothing will change or improve. In the past you might have weighed your pros and cons endlessly without getting on with your decision. Putting off a decision for a long time in order to understand all the ramifications can be too lengthy a process. Our experience is that it's better to make some decision sooner than to make the perfect decision later. What happens if you make a decision too slowly? In many cases, what was going to happen already happened, and unfortunately you were not in charge. That is a not desirable situation. If a decision does not turn out the way you expected, you can always make a course correction.

Here is my, Nina's, experiences, with making a first step and what came out of it.

For many months, I felt that I no longer was happy with my job. I did not enjoy the culture of the company. I started to realize I had to change my situation, but I had no clue what I wanted to do next or where to start looking. I felt exhausted just by thinking of having to look for a new job. The thoughts about updating my CV, looking for job openings, and understanding what I wanted almost paralyzed me. Due to the many working hours I needed to put into the job

I no longer liked, I also was exhausted with limited energy to be creative or take strong action. My thoughts about where to find a job at the same level with as good of a salary were very negative. I felt stuck, had no energy, and had no clue about where to start. So I just went on from month to month.

After a two-day internal strategy workshop, I finally realized that this no longer worked for me and that I had to make a decision to take action. At the end of the meeting I decided to reserve time first thing the next day to start looking for a new job. But, as it often happens when you do not really know what you want, I did not take action. A few days later, during a break between meetings, I started surfing on the internet for possible next steps. Since I had not kept up with the job market for years, it felt like a jungle, and pretty soon I felt trapped in negative thoughts and could not continue the focused search. Instead I started to search aimlessly on the internet.

I do not know how it happened, but all of a sudden I was on a homepage of a yoga and mindfulness center. I had never visited the center, but suddenly an eight-week mindfulness course caught my eye. It sounded really compelling, and before I knew what happened, I had signed up. The course started the very next day! This was my first mindfulness course ever, and attending the first session was a strong experience. It gave guidance to being in the present, letting your thoughts go, and being mindful. My concerns about my working situation made me sleep badly. In fact in the beginning, I fell asleep during the exercises, a true sign of how exhausted I was. Finding a new job still bothered me, but I decided that my first priority was to focus on getting to a better mental place and on better sleep.

Three weeks into the mindfulness course, I got a call out of nowhere from a recruiter who asked me if I would be interested in looking into an opportunity at the company I'd worked for earlier. It was a brand new role, and I said yes to an interview. After four weeks of different tests and interviews, I got a call from the hiring manager offering me the job! Wow! I got a job that suited me so much better with a great compensation package and at a company I really liked! The whole process was amazing! Instead of panicking and desperately trying to find a new job, I somehow understood that I was not in a good place to look for a new job. By taking that first step that felt good to me, things started to happen. Eight weeks after the start I finished the mindfulness course and had a new job! The process and the outcome were almost too good to be true. And I was in charge.

So, make a decision to take a first step, and things will start happening. If a decision turns out to be the wrong one, it can always be changed. But making a decision is the way to move forward, get new energy, gain momentum, and gain perspective. From there, the playground suddenly will look differently. Things that might have looked hard or impossible all of a sudden materialize.

To help you determine how you can go about making a decision to take that first step, here are some suggestions:

1. Ask yourself honestly why it's hard for you to take a first step.

2. One way of making progress is to understand where the most resistance lies in moving forward. Start with that task! When you have completed that task, the rest of the tasks will seem much easier.

3. Another way is to look at your whole situation. Could there be "low-hanging fruits" to get the energy flowing and change the conditions? A first step that makes the next feel possible?

4. Do something that you like and that gives you energy. It may have nothing to do with your situation or the problems you want to solve, but it gives you new perspective or inspiration. Nina's mindfulness course is a good example of this.

5. Is there somebody in your network you can be inspired by?

 Question to you:

In chapter 5 you will start creating your toolbox. Could this tool be one of the tools in your toolbox for change?

Tool 4: Allow Time and Space!

"I wanted to come here to be a human being and not a human doing," said Dave, a man we met on the camino.

We all go about making changes differently. Sometimes you consciously know what is wrong and how to get out of the situation. Other times you know you are frustrated, dissatisfied, and not in the place you want to be. You might want to change the situation, but doing so can be overwhelming. Your realization can actually cause you to feel even more trapped in the negative thoughts, relationship, or stuck situation you are in. How on earth will you have the energy and the courage to find the right timing to make a move? It might even be that you are in a good place but that there is something within you "that is knocking on your door to get attention," that is pushing you to start thinking that there might be a next level for you. However, you are not certain of what steps to take to begin your process of change. This is where allowing some time and space for yourself can be a great source of taking action. Yes, consciously allowing for some time and space is taking an action!

Elizabeth, an entrepreneur in a start-up business with several fascinating projects, expressed she felt so tired. She was not satisfied with her current situation, even though it was very creative and progressing very well. She said: "I understand I need a balance between doing and being. Actually I am better and I serve myself and others much better when I am being. And right now I don't have the balance because there is much too much doing!" In realizing what she was doing to herself, Elizabeth chose to take some time off to provide herself with a short period of spiritual focus and exploration. By the time she returned to her work, she was revitalized and was able to make some changes without impacting her productivity. She had brought on partners and had segmented her business activities in a logical manner that allowed for better focus. Since the measurement of much of our society is based on doing, it takes a conscious choice, a strong will, and urgency to stop and recharge, as Elizabeth decided to do.

We can compare this with companies that allocate time to focus on new initiatives. Google's "20% Project" allowed employees to spend 20% of their work week on new and creative projects. Most famously, Gmail emerged from this policy. Many companies allow and encourage focused time for creativity. Individuals should do the same, particularly when in a frozen situation.

Another example of this is Mary. *Mary was experiencing a nagging sense that she was missing the bigger picture and the greater calling in her life. She longed to simplify her life and to have her own time and space where she would not always be rushing in pursuit of the next business success. As a self-employed owner of a small business, she felt the demand to have her work take priority over all else. Her unease accelerated when a friend close to her age passed away suddenly of cancer and then her Mom shortly thereafter. Mary's mortality suddenly hit her in the face, and she* criticized herself for putting off the pursuit of many of her creative ideas and heart's desires for more than ten years.

One day Mary stumbled upon the film The Way with Martin Sheen and Emilio Estevez, about the Camino de Santiago, the thousand-year-old walking trail in northern Spain. It was a movie about a father's decision to finish the walk that his son had started but not finished due to his death while on the camino. Halfway into the movie, completely out of the blue, Mary said to her husband, "I need to walk the camino"! This truly came from nowhere since Mary did not know anything about the camino until then, nor had she wished to do any long walk. She began planning, and as she did, she began to experience a thrill at her core for this upcoming adventure in her life. Her soul seemed to be calling her to unplug from her daily life. During her year of preparation, she began to see ways to organize herself physically and mentally for the camino. She also started to glimpse how she could live more simply in her daily life at home with her family, friends, and her business.

Life on the camino is all about the simple life. One gets up in the morning and begins to walk a good distance for six to eight hours. As long as you follow the yellow arrows, you are on the right track. Mary spent almost six weeks on the camino, living a very simple life. The time and space allowed her to gain perspective and inspiration in dealing with her life back home. After this Mary was ready to make a big change. When talking with her about this, she said: "It could have been years before I had the clarity or readiness *to make significant changes if I hadn't given myself this break from daily life to walk the camino to ponder and experience how a truly simple life feels. I wanted to remain simple and uncluttered in my mind, body, spirit and material world, and I began to see what necessary actions I needed to take. Today I live a more simplified life and am more anchored in the present moment. It all started in a big way when I initially answered my soul call to the camino. I am so grateful and excited about what life changes I have been able to achieve! I have been able to organize and simplify my business life much better and by that I have more focused time with family and friends as well as for creative projects that I have postponed for so long. It also makes me happy that my experience has inspired some of my friends to take intentional time outs for introspection and make rewarding changes."*

Photo by Mary H-C

In this chapter we want to focus on the space you sometimes need to allow yourself to recharge, get clarity, and get ready to make a change. Often, we are able to execute changes linearly as the need occurs, but other times we just need to calm down and listen before we make a move. When you are in this place, you just need to trust the process. Trust that you are where you need to be and that you will "jump" or make the move when the time is right for you to create room for something new. We both have been in situations that did not work anymore, and we know from experience that even when someone is aware of their situation, they are not able to make a change until they are mentally ready. You must decide when it's time for you to make the change. Don't let anybody make you jump before you are ready! Action is king, but you are the one that has the power to say when and how!

Let's assume that you have "done your homework" and know that a change is needed. Sometimes you are totally ready and can go all in to the process of change. Other times your fear, your negative thoughts, and your limiting beliefs may kick in. One of my, Nina's, comforting life wisdoms comes from *Moominland Midwinter* by Tove Jansson, the Finland-Swedish novelist, painter, illustrator, and author of the Moomin books. In this book, Too-ticky, the sage of Moominvalley, says, "All things are so very uncertain, and that's exactly what makes me feel reassured." In times of uncertainty these words of wisdom inspire and calm me.

Make space for the change

You are now prepared to start making changes and dealing with decisions you need to make.

Even if you are prepared for and welcome these changes, you still need to make space for the new. This space between the old and the new can feel confusing. It might even feel like the saying, "It likely gets worse before it starts getting better." You will likely be removing things from your life, like assets, people, habits, activities, or traditions. In this phase it truly can feel like you are losing many things in your life, but actually you are creating space for something new. When you look at it as though you are creating new space, your mind will see the positive. At the same time, it is challenging since you still have not been able to clearly identify the new things, the new people, or the new opportunities that you are making space for. As we said earlier, it likely will get worse before it starts to get better. But suddenly, you will find yourself on a completely new level in life, when the new things that you made room for have started to kick in. It might feel like when you take off in a plane on a cloudy day. After a windy, bumpy start, you fly through the clouds and then, wow, there is the clear blue sky! Magnificent! Wonderful! Who could have believed it would look and feel like this on the new level!

Questions you can ask yourself:

1. Is there enough space for change in your life? Or are you rushing through your life? Are you truly making space for what is important to you?

2. Are you afraid of slowing down and dealing with your negative situation?

3. Are there specific environments, activities, situations or people that spark your energy and inspire you to think new thoughts and take new steps in life?

4. Do you know people who took a break in their lives and made positive changes following the break?

5. Can you start small? Doing small, positive things will give you an energy boost and inspire you to think and act in new ways.

 Question to you:

In Chapter 5 you will start creating your toolbox. Could this tool be one of the tools in your toolbox for change?

Tool 5: What Is Your Excuse?

How many times have you heard somebody saying: *I would have done this or that, if only...*? We create excuses for small things, like not regularly flossing, exercising enough, or eating healthy, as well as for more major issues like why we are not achieving our goals or why we remain in unwanted situations. Excuses are an efficient way of hindering you from taking action, taking a next step, or taking a chance. Excuses are great to hide behind when you don't feel strong enough to make the change even if you know you should. Why would we allow ourselves to make excuses to keep us from taking appropriate actions? What are the reasons why we make excuses? Let's look at some common excuses and then ways to deal with them.

Common excuses

1. Fear - *"I know I should take action, but am fearful of the unknown."*
2. Habit - *"I am so used to doing things this way."*
3. The Devil - *"The devil you know might be better than the devil you don't know."*
4. Comfort zone - *"I know I should act, but to do it might make me very uncomfortable."*
5. Timing - *"This just isn't the right time."*
6. Laziness - *"I don't really feel like doing anything today. Maybe in a day or two."*

7. Priorities -" *I have other things that I need to deal with first.* "

We know from our own and other peoples' experiences that excuses can hinder you from taking a next step, changing an unwanted situation, or taking actions necessary to get closer to your goal or intention. Excuses are tricky too, since a great friend of excuses is resistance. Maybe you have started to like your excuses. Maybe you are waiting for someone else to take control and solve the situation. Do you really want a change? Do you blame others or the circumstances or the timing for the fact that you are not taking a step and making a change? Any of these feelings can easily help us hide behind our excuses, rather than taking action. The longer we fill our lives with excuses, the more used to them we become and the more reasons we find to do nothing and even give up thinking about change.

How excuses can get in the way of change

When I, Nina, was in my 40s, I got a great opportunity to further develop my skills. I was given the opportunity to enter a two-year executive program. My challenge was that this would be in addition to my job and family responsibilities. The program was something I really wanted to accomplish! As I decided to move forward, I understood that I would need to change my way of doing things. I had a habit of postponing everything to the very last minute, always having a "good" excuse for that. My excuses would range from the great weather to not being in the right mood to other priorities, and I realized those excuses could not work for me any longer if I was going to be successful in my career. My desire to grow and develop was strong, so I promised myself that I would no longer let excuses keep me from this opportunity to develop. A great quote that helped me realize what I had to do and stick to my decision was this one from Henry Ford: "If you always do what you've always done, you will always get what you always got." *I decided to change my habit and was always early handing in my assignments. In my new approach, not only was I more timely, but I could also get a much better life balance due to my diligence in avoiding procrastination.*

After this experience I began thinking of my excuses in a new way. Today I think, yes, I have excuses and thoughts that try to stop me, but with my good experiences during my two years of studies, I know the value of not letting my excuses take over. If I hadn't wanted the studies strongly enough, it would have been easy to let my excuses stop me. I could have easily made excuses that let me procrastinate or convince myself that it was too hard to balance family, work, and my studies. So, ask yourself, do you want the change strongly enough? Today I look at my excuses for what they are and then deal with them.

People around you

Not only can your own excuses stop you, but people around you might also be hiding behind their excuses. It is hard to help someone who is stuck in their excuses. It can almost seem like that person has gone down in quicksand and cannot or does not want to get out of it. This is very frustrating to watch from the outside. Often when someone from the outside suggests a solution, the recipient of the advice strongly resists it. The person might even claim that they didn't mean their complaints and suddenly swear that all is well. This is very paradoxical. The act of complaining might almost have become a part of the person's personality. This can be a heavy burden for those who have to listen to the complaints, like family, friends, or colleagues. The complainer is providing excuses to make themselves feel better. In reality, their excuses just keep them stuck, instead of enabling them to take ownership and responsibility for their situation, as happened to Daniel:

Daniel is responsible for the sales department of his firm. He enjoys his work and colleagues, but every time you talk to him, you get the feeling he is minutes away from being burned out. Daniel always complains about how much work he has. Plus, his commute adds another two or three hours to his day, depending on traffic. When he is not working, he worries about all the things he will not be able to achieve.

One day, I, Terry, suggested to Daniel that he block one day off in his calendar where he could work from home. This would not just save him several hours that day, but it would also allow him to be focused with fewer interruptions. I reminded him that his company encourages people to work from home to reduce commuting and environmental impact. By doing this, he would also be setting a great example for his group. From my perspective, this would be such an easy first step for Daniel to change his situation, to get more balance in his life, and to achieve more in less time. Daniel agreed that this would be a good step, but he said it was not the best time for him to make such a change.

So, Daniel continues his old pattern. Now, every time I talk to Daniel, he shares the same story about too much work, the commuting time, and all the things he is unable to achieve. I worry that Daniel will soon be forced to make a much bigger change than simply working one day a week from home.

How can you deal with your excuse?

First, you need to find out what excuse is stopping you from making a move. Let's say that you are afraid of failure. This might cause you to not even try to apply for a job, take on a new position, or try out something new. When you have identified that you are afraid of failing, then you can start to examine that excuse by asking yourself questions like: What does failing look like? What is the worst thing that could happen? How would that impact you and your life? Is there truly a risk to fail or has your mind just made it up so you won't move out of your comfort zone? If you failed, could you learn something by that? These are just some questions you can ask yourself in order to uncover what is behind your excuses. Many times it's surprising to uncover the true reason.

You might even find that what you are afraid of is much less dangerous than the big scary shadows it is causing. As you begin exploring your excuses, you may discover that there is really nothing to be afraid of. In this regard, your excuses are a defense mechanism since they allow you to protect yourself from what you think or fear.

If you have identified that your excuses stand between you and your goal, you can start examining how much you really want something. How committed are you to achieving a certain goal, changing your career, or changing a relationship? For example, when I, Nina, wanted to become a groom of a horse, nothing could stop me — not biking the 25 minutes in bad weather to the stable or having to get up very early every weekend morning. Although it would have been easy to come up with excuses, I wanted my goal so badly that I wouldn't let them stand in my way. You can always find excuses, but by understanding how much you really want something, you can determine whether your excuses are just something to overcome or if they are telling you something else. In this case, you may not want something strongly enough and are not yet prepared for the effort.

This leads us to another way to deal with your excuses. After seeing the full picture, you might conclude that you are not willing to make the effort needed to change your situation. In this case, you might not make any visible changes, but you can accept the truth about your situation. This is a powerful method of dealing with your excuse since now you are making a conscious choice, rather than letting excuses take over.

To avoid your excuses taking control, you can question their validity. Are your excuses really accurate? For example, if your reason for not making a change is "I am too old," you can ask yourself the question, "Is that true?" Your first response might be, "Yes," but if so, then ask yourself, "What evidence do I have that this is in fact a valid concern, rather than just an excuse?" You might then discover that you are making excuses, hiding from some other issue. Maybe you are not really ready to make the effort to change your situation. Maybe your true fear is that you will not be able to find a better alternative, and you have decided to settle with the excuse "I am too old." By questioning your excuse, you might find the true reason behind it and then be much better equipped to make a decision based on the real reason.

Also, ask yourself if your actions take you closer or further from finishing a goal or making a change. When you decide on a change or set a goal, it's easy to let your excuses take over. You might spend time on Facebook or other social media instead of taking concrete action towards your goal. Remember to check if you are making progress. Do activities that get you closer to your goal while limiting or eliminating activities that keep you from your goal. The more observant you are about where your excuses take you, the better you will be able to deal with them.

Another way to avoid letting your excuses stop you is to understand what makes you feel good. What if you did more of what makes you feel good? Identifying that and implementing a daily feel-good routine can be an important first step toward change. Start growing the parts of your life that make you feel good, that give you energy, and that are positive aspects of your day. The more positive your daily life becomes, the more energy you will have to start dealing with the parts of your life you are not happy with. By doing this, you will feel ready to take new actions and grow. You will develop the understanding that the greatest hindrance is within yourself and not outside yourself. Understanding this is the first step to changing your situation and in the end changing your life.

Questions you can ask yourself to better understand your excuses and how they impact you:

1. What is your excuse? Do you know what your excuse really stands for?

2. Do you truly want to change your situation or have you settled behind your excuse?

3. Do your excuses keep you stuck? Do they comfort you so that you do not have to try to excel or change your situation?

4. What is the smallest step you can do today to take action despite your excuse?

5. Try to imagine what you would do if you didn't have this particular excuse. What would that mean? Who would you be? What would you do?

 Question to you:

In chapter 5 you will start creating your toolbox. Could this tool be one of the tools in your toolbox for change?

_____

Tool 6: Guilt – a Hindrance to Flow and Growth

The feeling of guilt can range from the smallest nagging feeling to an overwhelming, constant constraint. Guilt is a very powerful emotion that we experience when we believe we have caused harm to someone or something. Just believing we've harmed someone can immobilize us. The fact is that, whether or not our feelings of guilt are justified, they can neither change the past nor make us better people. So how can we move forward if we are stuck with our feelings of guilt?

We believe that guilt is inevitable in our lives. However, how we deal with our feelings of guilt is what is critical. Ideally, feeling guilt gives us the opportunity to learn from the past and get equipped to choose different behaviors in the future. However, when we do not or cannot constructively deal with our feelings of guilt and instead get consumed by them, we are hindered from living in balance and in the present moment. This can efficiently keep us stuck in the past. To avoid this, we need to understand why we feel guilty and then actively deal with our guilt. When we do this, it will allow us to make amends where appropriate, ultimately forgive ourselves, and then let the guilt feelings go. So how can we do this and be free to move on?

Guilt does not serve anybody, not you or the people involved. Remember, we all make mistakes. If you have done things that you feel guilty about, deal with them! If possible, talk to those who are involved. Be honest in your communication and seek forgiveness. If not possible to talk or act, then you need to find a way to forgive yourself and to let go. Our quality of life resides in our inner world, so the more we are possessed by our feelings of guilt, the more energy we give these feelings. When we understand this and can let go, the more peace we will feel. When freeing yourself from the feeling of guilt, you can focus on the present situation. You are then able to understand how the feeling of guilt has impacted you and how it has kept you stuck. With this knowledge and the new state of mind, you will be able to more clearly assess your current situation and take the right actions for you to move forward.

A few days before the end of the camino, we met Keith, a man in his 40s who was close to the end of his six-week-long walk. *For years Keith had constantly disappointed himself and people around him. Keith came to a point where he felt like a failure, and after a period of introverted living and heavy use of alcohol, Keith's sister convinced him to see a doctor and a therapist. As part of his treatment, individually and in counseling sessions, Keith started to reflect on his past. He began to understand that his feelings of loneliness and insecurity had to do with a grief that he had never dealt with.*

Keith's mother died from a car accident when he was only eight years old. The rest of his family seemed to move on in a healthier manner than Keith. Keith had a hard time finishing school, keeping a job, and remaining faithful to his partner. In his counseling sessions, Keith started to understand that his strong underlying feelings of sorrow, loneliness, and misery had kept him stuck with a diminishing picture of himself. His negative thinking of not being able to achieve things, to keep a job, and to be worthy of love seemed to fulfill itself, and problems seemed to gather around him. When Keith, after years of troubles, finally searched for professional help, he started to understand how much of his negative thinking and how many of his damaging behaviors actually came from his deep sorrow. He also understood that avoiding responsibility for his actions had become his way of dealing with important situations. Keith felt he had let so many people down during all the years of his negative and irresponsible actions. As he became more aware, it became critical for him to deal with his feelings of guilt.

This is the time he decided to go on the camino, to give himself time and space to reflect upon his life so that he could finally find peace with himself. The first days, Keith felt lost and alone and so far from home. After initial struggles, Keith started to enjoy his walk, as well as the talks with people he met. Day by day he grew physically and mentally stronger. A few weeks into the camino he came to the meseta, the flat plains on the plateau of central Spain. The meseta is considered by some as empty, flat, boring, and to be avoided. But it can also provide a great opportunity for deeper reflection and insight. A fellow pilgrim said, "The meseta is the toughest part to walk since it's so monotonous, but mentally it's the most rewarding part. This part of the camino can be a wonderful opportunity to empty yourself and create a new mindset. The perfect conditions to get your mind going!"

A few days into the meseta, Keith found himself on a walking meditation. The meseta became the turning point for him. Keith had by now reached a calmer state of mind and felt more in contact with himself. He dared to let the questions and thoughts that had tortured him so many times come to the surface. He was processing these and many other thoughts during his long days on the meseta. He was not able to set things right immediately, but now he had the courage to honestly look at his past. He knew what he had done and understood more deeply why he was thinking and acting the way he was. He had been self-sabotaging his life. He came to the insight and acceptance that he could not change the past, but now he had a great opportunity for a fulfilling future. If he continued to dwell on past actions and feeling guilty, there would be no room for growth and getting unstuck. After the camino, Keith was able to restart his life. As part of that, he reached out to the people he felt he had let down, explained himself, sought understanding and forgiveness, and came to peace with his life up to now. It was not easy, but consciously dealing with it made it possible for him to let the past go and start to take action based on his new insights and intentions for the future.

When guilt is what's keeping you stuck and you are worrying about the past instead of having the peace of the now, it's important for you to understand that guilt is a losing battle! It is an inner conflict that will keep you stuck in the past as long as you let it. Years, new opportunities, and new relationships can easily pass! Don't let this happen! Instead, accept yourself, your actions, and your history. Take actions to be forgiven, whenever possible. When you do so, you will be able to forgive yourself and can shut the door to that troubled part in your life.

Questions that can help you dealing with your feelings of guilt:

1. Do you know why you feel guilt?

2. Is your feeling of guilt valid, or are you judging yourself too hard?

3. How is your feeling of guilt impacting you?

4. How can you start dealing with the guilt? What is the smallest step you can take today to change your feeling of guilt?

5. How would you feel if you did not feel guilty and you were able to seek and get forgiveness and also forgive yourself?

 Question to you:

In Chapter 5 you will start creating your toolbox. Could this tool be one of the tools in your toolbox for change?

Tool 7: Deal with Your Fear

"Fear does not prevent death. It prevents life." – Naguib Mahfouz

Fear has an important function in our lives. It makes us aware of something that could be harmful to us. This is the good and natural side of fear. When fear starts inhibiting our daily lives, our choices in life, or our growth, it becomes the most powerful blocking factor in our lives.

My, Nina's, story about my fear is a combination of the obvious impact but also of the more hidden impact upon my activities and choices. As long as I can remember I have been afraid of flying. On a scale of one to ten, my fear has been at nine and a half. Before I decided to deal with my fear, the obvious hindrance to me was that I would travel less or always choose alternative ways of traveling, like train or boat. The more hidden aspect of this fear was that it impacted my career alternatives, and it almost stopped me from doing my executive studies because they required one trip from Sweden to the US. Becoming aware of both the obvious and the hidden impacts, I decided to start dealing with my fear. So I attended some private coaching lessons to help me overcome my fear of flying. In the beginning, it was not a pleasant experience since I needed to expose myself to the thing I feared the most, like flying from one destination to another as part of the coaching lessons. I also needed to break patterns that I had developed to cope with my fear, patterns that kept me thinking that flying was very dangerous. Facing the fact that my fear would have strong impacts on my choices in life, I finally dealt with it. I cannot say

I am a happy flyer (today maybe four on a scale of ten), but my fear no longer keeps me from planning my life or living my life the way I want to. My fear of flying no longer has the power to limit my life.

What fear does to us

Fear is one of the biggest reasons that people get and stay stuck. Fear can efficiently hinder us from opening up for new opportunities, people, and situations or from taking action, all of which limits our lives and potentially makes us feel stuck. Our fear can have very different faces and depth, but it can have the strongest power in keeping us frozen. It can cause us to avoid new experiences, give up dreams, or never dare to live our lives to the fullest. We can turn down opportunities that could be rewarding to avoid the risk of failing or hurting someone else. We can lose opportunities for something great because we are afraid to lose something else that only feels good enough. Maybe good enough is where we want to be, and we might choose to stay in what is comfortable. Here the important word is *choice*. When we make the conscious choice that this is what I want, then we are in control as opposed to our fear being in control. Facing and dealing with our fear gives us the opportunity for growth, happiness, and fulfillment.

Understand and deal with your fear

Have you identified that you are not happy where you are, that something no longer works for you, and that it's your fear that is preventing you from dealing with your situation? Where can you begin despite your fear? The first thing you need to do is to understand what you are afraid of. As you do this, it is important to be very specific. This way you can determine if it's a true fear, meaning that if it happened it would cause real damage to you and your life. If you think it would, it's important for you to understand and detail the implications. By knowing the implications, you are much more prepared to deal with them.

For example, if your biggest fears of leaving a relationship are that you would be lonely and that you would never be able to cope with that, then go through the whole thought process. If you want to separate or divorce, you are most likely already feeling lonely in your relationship. You might also have started to limit your joint social life as a couple. Feeling lonely in a relationship in many cases is a worse feeling than feeling lonely by yourself. So you might already have what you are afraid of in your relationship. If you were out of your relationship, you actually would be freer to act upon the feeling of loneliness — without the additional burden of the thoughts of separation or divorce also in your head. Your new situation would force you to think in new directions, and you could make decisions about what you want to have and do in your life, without taking into account the person in your relationship you want to leave. So in theory you might feel lonely when no longer in the relationship, but in reality you could feel liberated and have new energy to change your life.

When you know that what you fear would not cause real damage to your life, then you can detail what that fear stands for. Are you afraid of not measuring up to the new demands? Are you afraid of losing face or afraid of disappointing someone? You might even be afraid of being successful and what the change could bring with it! Sometimes you might fear that if you change one thing this change might cause an avalanche of additional changes. This fear might hinder you from even taking a small step because you fear you suddenly would be in the middle of a flood of changes that you cannot control. Or maybe you fear hurting someone because your choice could mean deviating from a plan that you had earlier set with them. Facing your fear, whatever it can mean, might be the last thing you want to do, but avoiding it does not make it disappear and will certainly hinder you from the next step in your life. It takes courage to do this, but that is the doorway to change!

Another important step in dealing with your fear is to understand what you are saying to yourself. Consciously or subconsciously, your inner voice is talking to you all day long, so understanding the quality of that talking is vital. Is the talk encouraging and positive or diminishing and negative? If your thoughts are *"I am scared to death to leave my job and start my own business,"* instead try starting the phrase with *"Part of me...":* *"Part of me is scared to death to start my own business, but part of me is really excited about the idea of running my own business in an area I love."* If you feel too scared to talk to your partner about how you no longer think your relationship works, you again can say, *"Part of me is so scared to open up about the difficult topic with my partner, but part of me is enthusiastic about what an honest and intimate discussion could lead to."* When you start listening and really observing what you tell yourself, you can sort out what parts of the talk you should pay attention to and what not to. In this process of listening, you will expose the limiting beliefs and negative thoughts and can actively foster positive, supporting beliefs. Understanding what you tell yourself and deciding how you want to view and act on it are highly important steps in changing your way of dealing with your fear.

Another important step is to understand that most of the things you fear will not happen. Most fears are like monsters in your mind. This attitude towards fear might sound too simple, but if you think back, you will most likely notice how little of what you feared throughout your life actually has happened. Maybe you'll also realize that if and when it did, you were able to deal with the situation much better than expected. Most of the time we are able to handle what we feared better than we ever would have expected. Based on years of experience, we have come to the understanding that worrying is most often merely a waste of time. When you can let go of worrying and scared thoughts, it will release a lot of energy, and you can start focusing on doing more of what you really want in life.

Love or fear

In his commencement speech at the Maharishi University of Management, Jim Carrey stated: "Fear is going to be a player in your life, but you get to decide how much. You can spend your whole life imagining ghosts, worrying about your pathway to the future, but all there will ever be is what's happening here, and the decisions we make in this moment, which are based in either love or fear."[8]

This is a powerful message about how much in our lives is based upon our choice between love and fear. They are two completely opposite thought systems. To Ann this became very clear when she realized she was stuck in a situation with a person who for years had been one of her closest friends.

Ann and her friend were very close and supported each other in the best and most loving way. When their life situations started to diverge, their relationship did too. At first small signs occurred, and Ann's friend would make comments about Ann's choices based on her own perspective and not out of a deep understanding and support of Ann. Then, Ann's friend started to show frustration with Ann and her decisions. Having been such close friends, Ann

8   www.youtube.com/watch?v=V80-gPkpH6M

took an unreasonably long time to understand that many of her friend's reactions and comments came out of her believing she knew what was best for Ann. She was acting as if her values should be Ann's values.

Normally Ann says what she thinks, needs, and wants. In this case, Ann was so afraid of losing the relationship that she became a pleaser. On her way to a more conscious life, Ann finally came to a point where she realized she did not want to have the kind of relationship they had anymore. Ann decided she would be willing to let her close friend go if they were not able to respect each other's choices and new ways in life. Ann understood that she, in her fear of losing the friendship, had started losing herself. Ann called her friend and said, "We need to talk about us." While walking to meet her friend, Ann felt peace within herself, knowing she could only win. The time had come to act out of love, not out of fear. Ann felt like a winner because she was true to herself, and she was letting love for herself and for her friend guide her, not fear. When Ann opened up, was honest, and showed her friend that she wanted her in her life, but in a new way, Ann's friend could also let go of her fear of losing Ann. That day a new kind of wonderful and honest friendship was born.

If you manage to keep avoiding things you fear, they will start to look scarier, and you will most likely be more and more afraid and work even harder to avoid them. But once you choose to deal with your fear, you begin growing. And the great thing is that when you have overcome a fear once, you know that you have the formula to do it again! You have experienced how overcoming your fear can take you to a new place, a new situation, and a better place for growth and happiness and you most likely will not let your fear stop you again to a point you would become stuck. When you are dealing with your fear, you are also setting an example. When you dare to do things despite your fear, you inspire others. When people around you see your courage, you show them a path where they also can make decisions based on love and not out of fear.

In the speech Jim Carrey gave to the graduating students, he talked about his father, who did not pursue his dream and failed. The quote he used was, "You can fail at what you don't want, so you might as well take a chance doing what you love."[9] This message is so worth considering. Go for the things that inspire you, things that make you feel happy and alive! If you fail, you at least tried. And there are always lessons to learn and potentially new opportunities coming up, even if the result was not what you thought it would be when you started. We encourage you to continue on the path that you intuitively know is yours, even if it's scary!

Here some tips how to deal with things you fear:

1. Detail and evaluate the negatives. What is the worst that can happen? Is that so bad? Make sure you detail the consequences so you understand how bad it is.

---

9   www.youtube.com/watch?v=V80-gPkpH6M

Maybe what you perceive as negative consequences actually could open up for new thoughts, happenings, people, and situations in your life.

2. Detail and value the positives that could come out of something you fear. Also remember to include the impact of doing nothing!

3. What gains are there in the long term by dealing with your fear, for you and also for others?

4. Visualize yourself still being afraid but handling the situation in an acceptable way. For me, Nina, visualizing myself flying — doing the procedure again and again in a calm and successful way — has helped me slowly handle my fear of flying.

5. Reduce your fear to something concrete or manageable. If your biggest fear is failing, then try to think, *"The thought of failing makes me very scared, but it would certainly not mean the end of my life."* As an example, one evening during a nice dinner, the host said, *"Let's compete in how many times you have gotten fired!"* It turned out that 80% of the participants had been fired one or more times. Actually the host himself, today a very successful CEO and co-founder of a tech company, had been fired four times! This little quiz helped to change the perception of failure. Failing actually is a part of growing and can lead you to something new and much better.

 **Question to you:**

In chapter 5 you will start creating your toolbox. Could this tool be one of the tools in your toolbox for change?

———————————

Tool 8: Find Your Passion

One day a friend of mine asked me, Nina, *"What would you do if you could not fail?"* What an opportunity! No possibility of failing? What is it that I would do? Sadly, I realized I did not know! I want to share the story how I was able to find my answer to the question:

Wilhelm, my son, did not enjoy studies in school. He had decent grades, but schoolwork was not something that he wanted to focus on any more than absolutely necessary. He was, instead, extremely fascinated with different kinds of computer games. In that area he was full of enthusiasm. He was eager to learn more and would save money to be able to buy the games he wanted. When Wilhelm heard about a high school with an emphasis on technology, media, and game development, he decided to go there. His first year was hard for him since writing essays and all types of extensive reading were not his interests. In the second year of the gymnasium, new studies like animation, coding, and game development were areas of focus, and suddenly he enjoyed school. Wilhelm was fully engrossed in these new subjects and quickly became very good in them. He was eager to learn and started to show great results. As he did well in these, he was more eager to do well in the areas that had not interested him the year before. It was amazing to watch the difference in his attitude towards his schooling.

In his third and last year, one of the big exams was to develop a computer game. Wilhelm and his classmate Philip started to develop a computer game and got more and more enthusiastic about it. They learned a lot as they struggled with it, but they stayed committed to the task. Despite the many hours they needed to put in and despite some setbacks, they stayed enthusiastic about their game. It was amazing to observe that even if this one big work was demanding, Wilhelm's overall results in his other classes continued to get better. It was delightful to follow him finding his passion. More than just playing games, he had developed the knowledge to create games.

When Wilhelm finished high school, he started to develop his first commercial computer game. After high school, most of his peers worked to earn money and traveled until the next year when they started university. However, Wilhelm stayed home, working in his room to develop his game. Much of the work at first was lonely, but over time he started to interact with his growing community. This community was an online global community that was following his game development and people he interacted with online. Even if some days were lonely, filled with boring trial-and-error tasks that had to be completed, he stayed focused on his passion. After hard months of work, he released his first game. The sales of it went very well, and his friend and former classmate Philip decided to leave university to join Wilhelm. This was how Landfall was started and Wilhelm is now living his dream! He has his own company in a field he loves, and he is surrounded by people he loves to work and spend time with.

To me, Nina, it has been a joyful and inspiring journey to follow Wilhelm's early steps of learning game development and then turning it into a true and innovative company. This has reminded me of what it truly means to find your passion and how rewarding it can be professionally and financially. This actually inspired me to dare to say yes to a voluntary leave package the company I worked for offered. I had loved my work and had successfully grown during my time with the company. However, I had begun to feel less motivated, so I decided to take that offer. Why? I started to hear a voice in me that asked if I was fulfilled with my life. That voice could have been asking me, "What would you do if you could not fail?" This growing unease in me, a growing dissatisfaction with my purpose in life, and the inspiration I got from following Wilhelm's journey made me make the decision to take the package.

Today, after walking the camino, travelling, and searching, I am able to tell what I would do if I knew I could not fail. What an amazing feeling! I acknowledge that it has taken me much longer than I thought to figure out what I really wanted. Many times, I questioned my choice to leave a well-paid job at a great company. I have also struggled with doubts about whether I am doing the right thing and wondering if this will lead to anything.

Wilhelm's choice not to go to a university to study but to sit at home all day and develop some computer game did not always make sense to the outside world. For those who could follow his journey closely, it was an easy decision to fully support him because he was so passionate and sure of his way forward. It was amazing to follow how he grew into his role from a student to a capable and inspiring CEO of a game development company in only three years. When Landfall released their third game, they had evolved from being a small group of guys working long days in Wilhelm's bedroom to a real company. They relocated and had become a hot start-up organization. This is when it became obvious to everybody that Wilhelm and his team had succeeded, big time! It had taken Wilhelm three years to get to the point where he could be considered a success by the outside world.

Now back to me and my thinking. Three years is a long development time, a long time staying focused, passionate, and committed on your end goal. I began to understand that development times can be very long. It is much easier to allow yourself the development time when you have a clear goal, like Wilhelm. But when you know you are dissatisfied with what you are doing but have doubts about your ability to do something new, how do you proceed? It starts with reviewing in your heart and soul about what you feel your passion and maybe even your purpose is. Today, I clearly can answer, "I know exactly what I would do if I could not fail!" The answer is, "What I do today!"

I am now focusing on what is important to me, which is helping people grow. How did I finally get there? I found my "Spotify-energy"!

In the long days and weeks when nothing seemed to happen to give me more clues about what I wanted as a next step in my life, I got energy identifying that I wanted to work for Spotify, the highly innovative, entrepreneurial company with a product people love. I got the energy to start looking for ways to become employed by Spotify, and because of the actions I took, things started to happen.

New people started to show up in my life, and new opportunities started to present themselves. By finding the first and real spark to something new I wanted, I got energized and inspired to continue the work of finding my passion. For me a passion for what I am doing has always been important, be it horses, the studies I chose, or workplaces. This new step was different. It would impact my whole life in a much broader way! I understood that working with something really meaningful and owning my time were two non-negotiable parts of my new life. Because of that, I needed to understand how I could turn what I loved — personal growth, helping others growing, working in an entrepreneurial and high energy environment — into something that I could do for my living.

How can you find your passion?

Some people know what they love in life and are fortunate enough to do what they love to do. They have found their passion. We see passion as when you have a powerful and compelling feeling that creates strong energy in you. It is the feeling of being in the flow. We believe it's important to have a feeling of flow in one's life, even if you cannot pursue your passion full time. Whether it is sports, literature, vocation, travel, relationships, gaming, networking, or music, it is important to find an area that gives you happy energy. When you have that in your life, many other things will go so much more easily. It's a great platform to operate from and make changes from.

If today you do not have that happy energy, a first step is to start thinking of what that could be. You might wonder, *"Why should I have to find my passion? Shouldn't it just come by itself, since it's a passion?"* If you already know your passion, then, yes, you just can focus on maintaining and growing that space in your life. But many people struggle with identifying their passion, especially when they are feeling stuck. If that's the case for you, then the first thing you can start with is to think about your life, your whole life up until now.

When have you been in situations when you have felt happy, full of energy, and as if you are in the right place? Think of one, then think of the next, think of as many situations as possible. Write them down and see if you can see a pattern. Then start to look at your findings in more detail. Is it a special environment, role, geography, activity, co-operation, or health-related activity or situation that you can identify as the carrier of the good feeling? When you have made some more findings, then you can start combining these with how you would like to bring this kind of energy into your life. Is it into a new career, new relationship, new role, hobby, or even way of living? When you have identified this, you can start focusing on specific ways to grow happy energy in this area. The more things you really like in your life, the more likely you are to grow them even more, and the less likely you are to get or stay stuck.

When you open up for something new and start to take action towards it, things will start coming your way. Just like Nina when she found her "Spotify-energy." To develop, to change, to grow, and to fulfill your passion, you will need to take some risks. You will need to cope with rejection and maybe failure. There might be times when something happens that makes you put your pursuits on hold. This is part of the journey, and as Tony Robbins, the American bestselling author and life success coach, says: "The only problem we really have is we think we're not supposed to have problems! Problems call us to higher level — face & solve them now!"

The quote that has helped me, Nina, is, "As I look back on my life, I realize that every time I thought I was rejected from something good, I was actually being re-directed to something better," by Steve Maraboli, the life-changing American speaker and bestselling author. This has proven itself right so many times in my life. Even if disappointed at times by unwanted change, rejection, or a failure, I have been able to reevaluate the specifics and redirect myself for the better. So when you find your passion, what gives you energy, what makes your day, and what makes your future worth longing for, go with it! As Oprah Winfrey, the American bestselling author and media leader, says, "You get in life what you have the courage to ask for."

By the way, I did not get a job at Spotify, even though I tried many formal and informal ways, like sending mail directly to the CEO.

*I even shared my affirmation picture with him, which is a picture
I had created to help me stay optimistic and energized about my
chances to get to work for Spotify. When talking about my great
wish to work for Spotify, a person said, "Why are you limiting
yourself to Spotify!? Ride on the energy, the great feelings, and
the passion you feel by thinking about Spotify. Take that warm,
inspiring Spotify glow and do something about it that is you!"
And I did! I have followed my Spotify-energy and transformed
my life into what makes me happy. I am now a published author,
I am co-founding an app that helps people gain more insight, and
I am doing something that is meaningful to me while positively
impacting others! I have not updated my CV with all this, but I
figured that if what I do now does not turn out as planned, I have
learned a lot during the journey, figuring out what my passion is,
and following it. Who knows what one day will happen with me
and Spotify!?*

 Question to you:

In Chapter 5 you will start creating your toolbox. Could
this tool be one of the tools in your toolbox for change?

Tool 9: Discover What You Want

You have now learned about many different tools you can use. You can change your inner voice and you can also think about how you deal with your barriers, like fear or guilt. But what about your overall direction? Do you know where your yellow arrows are pointing? Do you have a clear view of your desires and direction in life? This is one additional area of thought that we believe is critical for moving forward. This is important also in order to avoid stuck situations.

Intention

There is a saying: "People plan for their next vacation in more detail and with more clarity than they plan for their lives." For most people, a vacation is a joyful and inspiring thing to think of and to plan for. They develop a concrete plan with some firm steps, like picking a starting and ending date, booking transportation, and establishing a clear destination or road map for the journey. Do we do the same when it comes to our lives? Isn't the most important and inspiring task we as individuals have to establish a clear view on what we want in life? Without that, it's like wanting to go on a vacation but not having a clear idea about when and where you want to go. Without that clarity, you would likely end up staying home and being frustrated over not getting away. That would be a very frustrating situation, but isn't that how it is in life too without a clear intention?

An example of having a clear life intention is Ty, a global healthcare entrepreneur. His intention is twofold. His first and immediate intention is simply to be happy every day. His second and broad intention is to successfully impact the health of thousands of cancer patients through early diagnosis and treatment. *"My daily happiness is gained by getting the things done that I want to get done each day. I don't want to be in a position where I try to do so much each day that I get frustrated. My happiness serves as a great ongoing indicator that I am on track. For the bigger decisions, both when to say yes and when to say no, my intention to impact people's health regarding cancer serves as my clear yellow arrow."*

When talking about what you want in your life, one can use words like vision, intention, and purpose. We have decided to use the word intention, since it's more actionable than vision or purpose. We define intention as a powerful statement that describes what you want to achieve or be. If other words resonate better with you, don't get too hung up on the definition but focus instead on the goal of this chapter — to help you gain a clear view on your life.

Why have a life intention?

Determining your life's intention gives you a clear view of where and what you want to be and what you want to do. It will help make your yellow arrows visible and guide you through life's changes and challenges. With this in place, you can more easily avoid being stuck. When talking about this, most people recognize the benefit of having an understanding of what they want in life, but do not write down their intention. Written or not, clearly identifying what you want in life is important.

When talking to Clare, a retired teacher, about having an intention for one's life, she said: *"I wish I would have been more adventurous in my life and that I would have had an intention for my life. When I stopped working, I wish I would have dared to live more for the day and not just stay in my little town. If I would have raised my eyes towards an intention for my life, not living day by day or week by week, I might have caught that I wanted to experience living in a new country, being more adventurous and taking a few more risks. After my retirement I had the financial security to do that, but I did not. That is something I regret, and defining my intention would have helped me see that."*

This discussion motivated Clare to think about her life intention. Next time when discussing this she triumphantly said, *"I have made a life intention! I used to be a teacher all my life. Now I want to learn, so I have enrolled in a Spanish course. I will not move anywhere else. I love my little town, but I want to join a group of people who I know spend some months in Spain escaping the darkest and coldest time here. So, by learning Spanish, I will feel more like living in a new country, not just visiting, and then when back at home, I will be enjoying my life here even more since I now get both worlds. I feel really excited about my path forward!"*

Another reason to have a clear intention is that it can help you make decisions today, tomorrow, next month, and next year. It will also give you a basis to help you prioritize and understand what is important in the short term as well as in the longer perspective. An example of this is Sven, whose overall intention is to live until he is over 100 years old. Today he is 47, and knowing that he wants to live a fulfilled, healthy, and sustainable life for more than 50 years to come, he can prioritize his daily, as well as his long-term, decisions. *"I do not need to stress decisions that do not come easily. When it comes to work, my plan is to work at least 40 more years, so that puts things into perspective for me. When it comes to health, I eat and exercise in a way that is good for my body also in a long-term perspective."*

Intention evolves just as life does

Will our life intention change over time as our life evolves? Absolutely yes. Major components of it will remain, but the emphasis from one aspect to another might change. This is natural, since life changes do occur. If one sticks to an intention that doesn't account for life changes, then one can get dissatisfied or even stuck. Therefore, flexibility to life's changes must be a part of the process. Terry offers a good example of how life intentions evolve. He went from being focused on creating a family, developing a career, and making money to being focused on his passion for health care and maintaining a great balance between work, family, and adventure. Here are Terry's intentions and how they have evolved throughout different stages of his life:

Early Adulthood intentions

1. Begin a family and create a home and family environment similar to my upbringing.
2. Make enough money to support my family.
3. Become a leader in healthcare where my passion for helping people and leading others could be fulfilled.
4. Maintain an active focus on health and exercise.

Mid-Life Intentions

1. Grow leadership impact in healthcare.
2. Lead a more balanced life relative to time with family, friends, and hobbies.
3. Financial growth.
4. Maintain active focus on health and exercise.

Pre-Retirement Intentions (current)

1. Greater balance. Go to 50% work time. Focus is on healthcare through being a member of several company boards as well as doing strategic consulting.
2. Focus on love, family, friends, world travel, and personal health.
3. Financial security.

4. Be an inspiration, role model, and mentor to others.

Retirement Intentions

1. 20% work time in healthcare.
2. Continue focus on love, family, friends, travel, and personal health.
3. Be an inspiration, role model, and mentor to others.

My, Nina's, intention has changed a lot through the last two years. *When I left my structured working life, I did not have an outspoken intention. Life just rolled on. When I started to feel less fulfilled in my job and with my overall life, I was lucky and maybe brave enough to take the chance of getting a break. Through this transition, my desire to have a clearer basis for my choices in life has grown. One of the big reasons I decided to leave my last job was that I did not feel that what I did was meaningful to me anymore. Subsequently, my intention has evolved from finding a meaningful job to being more in tune with who I am and what I want in life. Today my intention is: I want to own my time and work and live wherever I want to. I want to continue growing as a person and help people grow. I want to feel passion in my life, both when it comes to the people in my life and the way I live and contribute.*

The above intentions illustrate different kinds of life intentions. Some are very broad, and some are much more specific, evolving with experiences and age. Much has been written about the various approaches to creating a life intention, and it's up to each of us to determine which approach is best for us.

Developing your life intention

Our experience is that developing a life intention, whether short or long term, is demanding, but can be highly rewarding. If we take the time to tune in to ourselves, we can get in touch with our inner self and begin to understand what we truly want. Whatever period of time is the best for you, doing this will help immensely in taking you to concrete next steps in your life. What if, by doing this, your whole life starts to feel like a great vacation? When you plan your life more than you plan your vacation, you can pack your life bag with the right items for you, and you will have your own clear arrows when you take off on your new road!

Here some questions that can help you get started with your intention:

1. Do you have a plan for your next six months, a year, or a few years? Why not? How could you benefit from having a clear sense of the next steps to take and goals to reach by a certain time, to help you get from your frozen situation?

2. Do you know your values? Our individual intentions are strongly influenced by our values, including areas like integrity, passion, equality, contribution, respect, honesty, or independence. You may be aware of your values, or they can be just implicit. Consider how combining your values with an intention could benefit your life.

3. How would it feel if you had an overall intention for your life?

4. Do you know good examples of people who have a clear intention for their life?

5. Can you get their help or inspiration when reflecting and creating your own?

 Question to you:

In Chapter 5 you will start creating your toolbox. Could this tool be one of the tools in your toolbox for change?

Tool 10: Resources - Additional Sources for Help

While all of our tools could be considered resources, we also have the opportunity to turn to friends, mentors, and role models to assist us as we look to getting unstuck. Many people feel that they should be self-sufficient and be able to deal with their unique issues. They might fear looking vulnerable, are shy, or do not know who to turn to or where to turn to get help. It's important to seek support when you need it. It is likely that you can get the clarity and additional input you are seeking from others, many of whom likely have experienced what you are now experiencing.

The first part of this chapter focuses on what forms of human support can be invaluable as we work to transition from our negative situation. The key human resources we will share include friends, mentors, role models, and a sounding board. In the second part of the chapter, we will suggest different kinds of resources, like books, TV shows, a podcast, and an app we use.

Friends

Friends can include any individuals whom you consider trustworthy and caring and who know you well. There is an intimacy in these relationships that allow for familiarity and mutual knowledge of each other, usually over a prolonged period of time. When you feel frozen, friends might be the first source of help you turn to, especially if you have friends that are great listeners. Many times it's a big help to be able to express your feelings to someone, no matter how unstructured, unclear, and negative your thoughts are about your situation and your ability to change it. When you are able to share your thoughts on what is keeping you stuck, you can get input. An insightful friend can ask questions that can guide you to more clarity, can challenge you, and can also inspire you. Your friends might even, when appropriate, help you access their network or other resources you could need.

However, some of your friends might be challenged by the transition you are experiencing and, because of that, give you advice that keeps you in the position you want to get out of. They might project their own fear on you or challenge you in a negative manner that becomes a hindrance to your growth. It's important for you to understand where they come from when giving you advice. The friends you need are those who understand and are sympathetic to your overall situation and who will listen to you, inspire you, and sensitively challenge you.

Mentor

Another resource to discover and cultivate is a mentor. You may not know this person well, but you should be comfortable approaching them. To test the waters, you would first share that you respect and appreciate what this person has done or what the person stands for. Then, ask the person to share some of their thoughts on how they have achieved their intentions. As that conversation continues, you will either feel comfortable in being more candid about your situation, or you will not. If not, keep looking for the right mentor. This is a relationship that needs to continue over a period of time, not just one or two meetings. Most individuals whom you would consider successful in an important area for you would love to support you and your development.

Role model

Closely related to the mentor approach is to find an inspiring role model. This would be a person who has succeeded in a way that resonates with you. This could be someone who dared to follow their dream or a person who inspires you by embracing life and inner peace. It could be someone who dared to say yes to a big career move despite the risk of failure or someone who, after years of being alone, opened up for a new relationship in life. Sometimes you know this person, but if you don't, you would still be able to learn and be inspired by following this person on social media or other means.

Sounding board

An additional human resource tool we suggest is a more formal structure that can involve friends, peers, or people from your network you respect and trust. In this model, you will wish to bring various talents to the table as a committee to learn about you and your issues. The group will discuss possible solutions, and the members will then support you in assimilating the discussion and developing your action plan. In this more formal structure, it is normally incumbent upon you to give them your plan of action, as well as regular briefings on your progress, and then allow them to give you ongoing input. This formal action plan should be given to your board with specific actions and dates. This might be an extensive and even scary process for you, but the benefit and progress you will experience are worth the effort.

I, Terry, used the sounding board approach several years ago. I had moved from a senior management career path to be co-founder of a high-tech start-up company. After four years, the company was progressing such that I felt I could leave and go back to my passion of healthcare. However, most recruiters felt I would be going backward if I took the types of leadership positions I desired. But I knew the area I loved. After feeling particularly frustrated at my lack of progress, I decided to bring together several of my friends and former peers who were also leaders in the healthcare industry. With their guidance, support, and contacts, I was able to get great input and also had a group that would network on my behalf. Within five weeks, two great leadership opportunities were presented to me. I took one of them, and my career was once again on track according to my passion.

It is appropriate to mention additional resources that can be of great help, depending on your beliefs and financial capabilities.

We are referring to the clergy or professional counseling. Depending on the issue you are confronting, these resources could be vital to you.

The use of any one of the above resources will be dependent upon the issue that is making you stuck. They can be related to career, mindset, relationships, health, crisis in beliefs, life vision, and others. Depending on the depth of the issue, you will lean towards one or a combination of the resources above since the feedback you will receive can be more or less meaningful, depending on the abilities of people involved. Remember, it is your willingness to open up and share in order to get feedback that will allow you to become unstuck.

Other resources

Here we want to share a few of the resources that have helped us during different times in our lives.

Books

We start with books since we strongly believe books can change lives.

Finding peace in the now. *The Power of Now* by Eckhart Tolle

For us, the most powerful book in times of being stuck, feeling unsettled, worried, sad, or in a feeling of deep frustration has been *The Power of Now* by Eckhart Tolle. When going through some tough times in life, the message of this book has been a savior. Even in the hardest times, you have the possibility to be in the now and to find peace in the now. *The Power of Now* gives you the tools and the reasons to find your inner peace. When you do this, you can rest and recharge, and your thoughts will be clearer. This process leads you to your own best place.

Focusing your thoughts on what you want in your life. *The Secret* by Rhonda Byrne

This book has been a vital guide to understanding the impact of our thoughts. According to *The Secret*, our thoughts and feelings attract a corresponding energy to ourselves, based on the fact that like energy attracts like energy. In short, what we focus on we will attract more of that into our lives. The central message of *The Secret* is that we have the power to change and create our life and our future.

A valuable, easy-to-read book about change. *Who Moved My Cheese?* by Spencer Johnson

Life changes constantly, and the better we understand the mechanics of change, the better we can deal with change. When you feel stuck, this is a book to get more insight about the process of change, what kind of role you have in the process, what role you could have in it, and how to better deal with change. *Who Moved My Cheese?* is very easy to read and to understand.

Meditation

Meditation is a way to calm your mind, find peace, center in the now, reduce anxiety, and build self-confidence. Research by Massachusetts General Hospital found that meditation changes the brain after just eight weeks of meditation. The study showed changes in different areas of the brain, including growth in the areas associated with memory, sense of self, empathy, and stress regulation.[10]

There are many sources of meditation to be found in different media. We recommend the free app **Insight Timer.** *Insight Timer* is a meditation app that contains approximately 4000 guided meditations in many different languages. If you want to create your own meditation, there is also a timer function where you can develop your own meditation.

On Being

On Being is an award-winning public radio conversation and podcast. *On Being* opens up the questions at the center of human life: What does it mean to be human, and how do we want to live? *On Being* takes up the big questions on

---

10   www.washingtonpost.com/news/inspired-life/wp/2015/05/26/harvard-neuroscientist-meditation-not-only-reduces-stress-it-literally-changes-your-brain

the meaning of life with scientists, theologians, artists, and teachers. www.onbeing.org/podcast

TV-shows

MarieTV

MarieTV is an online weekly show hosted by Marie Forleo, an American life coach, motivational speaker, author, and web television host. *MarieTV* contains hundreds of episodes with discussions and ideas to help you create a business and a life you love. Episodes focus on topics ranging from "Build a Meaningful Business," "Find Clarity, Passion, and Purpose," and "How to Re-Program Your Subconscious Mind to Get What You Want"

www.marieforleo.com/marietv

The Inspiration show

The Inspiration Show is an online show hosted by Natalie Ledwell, a motivational speaker and a bestselling author. In *The Inspiration Show*, Natalie interviews thought leaders in personal development and everyday people with inspiring stories from all over the globe. As of today, there are more than 450 short inspirational shows. Topics include "How to Transition through Big Life Changes," "How to Organize Your Life," "Discover Your Talents in Five Steps," and "How to Find Spiritual Fulfillment," just to mention a few of the shows. www.theinspirationshow.com/

Other sources for help are **world-famous thought leaders** like Tony Robbins, Oprah Winfrey, and Deepak Chopra, all found on different media like YouTube and Twitter.

On **TED Talks** you can find insightful, inspiring, and helpful talks under the topic of personal growth. www.ted.com/topics/personal+growth.

 **Question to you:**

> In Chapter 5 you will start creating your toolbox. Could this tool be one of the tools in your toolbox for change?

Now you have learned about the 10 actionable tools to assess your situation and take action. You have learned how we and many others have dealt with our situations of being stuck, whether that feeling came from our mindset, fear of the unknown, fear of hurting others, or maybe a feeling of no direction in life. Until now, we have presented the tools one by one. Many times, however, you need to use a combination of tools to deal with your situation. In the next chapter you will learn about four life stories and the different tools that were used in each of them. By reading this we hope that you will get even more encouraged to start building your own toolbox.

Chapter 4

A Special Discussion
on Lost Love

What are the most significant issues that can affect our lives? Certainly serious illness or death are foremost in our minds when we think of what can turn us upside down in life. Right behind these is that area that can make us indescribably happy or grief-stricken. We are referring to love relationships. We all know from our friends, family, and ourselves that the loss of a major love causes people to feel stuck more than anything else. In this chapter we will share the stories of Thomas, Laura, Anna, and Linda. As part of each of the four stories, we share the tools they used to deal with their respective situations, to find ways to move on, and to create a new direction for their lives.

We are focusing on loss of love here since this relates to the many times one "loses in love" for one reason or another and becomes frozen or stuck. When we believe that we have found our "one true love," we rejoice in our life each and every day. We also are confident that this love will last "forever." Wonderful it is, when that happens! However, too many times, something happens, or cannot happen, that takes that relationship off course, and it ultimately ends in pain, disappointment, parting of the ways, or a redefinition of that love relationship. When this happens, no matter how explicit or implicit the warning signs are, we might feel devastated, betrayed, hurt, and suddenly lost in our lives and future intentions. Wherever our yellow arrows have been leading us to, we are now lost in a fog that we cannot penetrate with our eyes. Our broken hearts have taken over our lives.

Lost love is something most people experience. You might have been left by your love and life partner, you might not dare to leave a partner because you think he or she could not cope with it, or you might be stuck in a situation where you just cannot let go of what you thought your relationship was. You might be in a situation where you know you will hurt your partner who deeply loves you, but your relationship has become damaging to your mental or physical health. We have dedicated this chapter to how lost love can painfully impact our lives and how we can lessen the negative impact this can impose upon us, from both length of time and emotional depth.

Life is too short not to love!

Thomas and his wife had a good marriage, but as years passed by, their focus was much more on their three children, their hobbies, their jobs, the house, the garden, and all the different home projects than on their relationship. The relationship change happened so slowly that it was hard to recognize the depth of the change. In time, they hardly spoke about personal matters anymore. Neither did they spend focused time as a couple. The intimacy and fun they once had shared was gone. Yes, they did make some attempts to bring back intimacy and improve communication, but other things always seemed to be more important than their relationship. So Thomas focused on his things and his wife on hers.

Thomas became very dissatisfied and truly wanted a strong and loving relationship, and it was becoming more and more difficult for him to cope with the lack of connection, engagement, and intimacy between him and his wife. One Friday afternoon he found himself sitting in the car, not wanting to go home after work. Thomas just drove around for hours with his mind spinning like crazy. He had come to a point where he could no longer "play the male role in a film or company called Family!" This reaction seemed to come like a bolt from the blue! He became breathless when he visualized his current pattern of many nights without sleep, his low level of energy, and his total lack of enthusiasm for their coming vacation or for the future.

As his reality became conscious, Thomas immediately began to think of divorce. However, this triggered thoughts about what he would lose. What about their many years of family traditions, their comfortable life, and the wonderful house? How could he possibly think of losing or risking all that!? But what about the long life ahead of him? Was life only to exist and let time pass? Was not life meant to be so much more? Something in him told him that life is too short to not love! He was breaking out in a cold sweat asking himself these questions. But he had no answer. He felt totally stuck!

One day, months later, he summoned the courage to share his situation with a friend. The friend was very surprised to hear about the poor relationship, but indicated he had noticed that Thomas was not the energized and outgoing person he used to be. He asked Thomas a few questions, the first one simply was, "How long has it been like this in your life?" At first Thomas could not believe his answer — "More than four years" — but he realized this was the truth. The next question was, "How much does it cost you in not dealing with this situation?" As Thomas pondered this, he came to realize that the cost was incredibly high in terms of emotional stability and life fulfillment. For years he had not dared to truly look at his and his wife's relationship. He was so afraid to lose everything they had built over the years. He started to clearly see that, instead of dealing with his love relationship, he had initiated many home improvement projects hoping to change the dynamics of the relationship. He understood that until now he had not been ready to face the fact that the love relationship between him and his wife was not at all as it used to be.

When leaving his friend, Thomas surprisingly felt a glimmer of hope. He had reached the point when he knew that he had to choose between being stuck and unfulfilled versus sharing true thoughts with his wife and all the risks that would bring. When he drove home from meeting with his friend, he made the decision to have an honest discussion with his wife. If she was not willing to jointly start working on changing their relationship, he finally would be ready to trade off years of a poor relationship for a divorce.

When Thomas took that first step by being honest about his feelings for his wife and their joint future, her first reaction was denial. She did not admit to the lack of communication and intimacy between them but she agreed to see a counselor with Thomas. The first sessions of counseling did not make a noticeable difference but as the sessions continued, the relationship between Thomas and his wife started to change. The first signs of that was that they were able to communicate in a new and more intimate way. They also realized that they had focused far too much on material and practical things rather than on maintaining and nurturing their love relationship. The big change in how Thomas viewed their joint future came the day he found himself whistling on his way home, feeling very excited about the coming weekend getaway with his wife.

These are the tools Thomas used:

Resources: Thomas sought help from a friend, a resource he could trust in this specific matter.

Deal with your fear: Thomas had for so long been driven by his fears of losing his relationship with the kids and the comfort of home and traditions. But in truly analyzing the cause of his fear, he realized he would lose more if he didn't take action.

Make a decision to take a first step: After all that time in limbo, Thomas made a bold decision to truly open up to his wife and accept the consequences, even if that meant letting go of the marriage and their way of living.

Resources: Thomas and his wife met a counselor who was able to help them start communicating again. This was the first big step towards the change in their relationship. The next was that they understood they both wanted to invest in their relationship and do all they could to find a way back to the loving and fun relationship they once had.

You need to let go!

We met Laura on the camino. She had been going through a major transition in her life and told her story about lost love. A few years earlier when Laura was newly divorced, she met Richard. He was the total opposite of her former husband. He was communicative, loving, and adventurous, all very important traits to Laura. Laura and Richard fell passionately in love.

There was a problem, however. He was married. From the very beginning of the relationship with Laura, Richard claimed that he and his wife were already in the process of getting divorced. Laura felt she had met her soul mate. After some wonderful and fun times, Laura wanted to know Richard's plans for his divorce and how he saw their future. Richard assured her that he wanted to continue his life with Laura, and they started to dream of their life together, including having children.

Despite this, Richard showed no real signs of changing his relationship with his wife. Laura was deeply in love with him but worried that he was not being honest. These fears started to torture her, and after sleepless nights she gave Richard an ultimatum: either get divorced or it was over. Richard continued to stall and make promises, which time and again turned out to be empty. Laura vacillated from feeling excited and optimistic to worried and distrustful. After several weeks, Laura realized that perhaps there was no right timing for Richard!

With a bleeding heart, Laura broke up with Richard. The days and weeks that followed were a nightmare for her. All she could do was think about Richard, whether she had done the right thing, and what he was doing. She was unable to focus on anything other than her work and her sorrow over the lost love, lost friendship, and lost future with Richard. Over and over again, she recalled her times with Richard, from first meeting and falling in love to the tough weeks where she started to understand he was not going to make the changes in his life that he had told her he truly wanted.

Months later, Richard contacted her and said he and his wife had now separated, and he wanted to meet. First, Laura was cautious, but Richard was very convincing. Laura finally agreed to meet. Laura was ecstatic as they met, but as the evening went on, she could feel Richard was not fully there. Richard assured her of his love and how much he had missed her, but when Laura wanted *to know his detailed plan for the divorce and for them as a couple, Richard again became unclear. The evening that started with great hopes for the future instead ended in total pain, and Laura once again had to say goodbye to Richard. Not only was Laura feeling sorrow and pain, but also a feeling of failure. How could she, an insightful and smart woman, have believed Richard again?*

Laura became totally stuck in her sorrow. She wondered how she would be able to move on from this situation, how she would survive the loss of this love, and how she would ever find joy again. A few weeks later, Laura happened to meet an old friend whom she had not seen for a long time. She told her story. Her friend looked at her and said: "Laura, I know exactly what you are going through. Its hell, and I feel so sad for you. I know how you love this man and how sad you are for the relationship and future you thought was to come. Yes, he was a great match and a strong passion, but if he is not ready to start a life with you and be your partner in life, then you need to let him go. So as hard as it is, as much time, thoughts, and energy you feel you have invested in this, you need to let him go, and you need to move on. Otherwise you might be in waiting mode for the coming months and maybe even years. Is this the kind of love and respect you want to give yourself? Do you really want to pause your life and maybe miss a lot of new opportunities and even finding someone new you love? Is that what you want for yourself!? It is past time for you to start to focus on your new life and what matters to you. If not, years might pass and you will become bitter. Trust me. This happened to me, and after far too many years, I have managed to let the man go and am slowly building a new life."

Laura was so thankful for having met her old friend and the unexpected insight she could give her. The change in Laura did not happen overnight, but a seed had been planted. She had started to understand that no matter how much she loved Richard and how wonderful their future could have been, there was nothing to build on if she was the only one committing to their relationship. As an act of respect for herself, she finally was able to make a decision to let go. Making this decision was essential for Laura in order to start creating and living the life that she wanted to live.

Today Laura is living a very happy life. As part of building her new life, she explores new hobbies, one of which is trekking in the mountains. This new passion of hers has taken her to many places on earth. She also decided to do the camino as part of her new life. This is where we met her. We found her to be a joyful and lively person who has found her peace. She was full of excitement for her new hobbies, the home she had bought, and for a person she just met before going on the camino. Laura was happy to share her story since she knew of so many people who had been in similar situations, and she also knew how much the advice of her old friend had meant to her.

These are the tools Laura used:

Resources: The insightful words and advice from Laura's friend provided the insight to start the process of change and letting go.

Make a decision to take a first step: Laura did not know where or how to start, but she made the decision that she would not allow Richard to damage her life anymore. This first decision allowed her to take some new steps, which included finding activities that inspired and energized her, like trekking and hiking. After the first decision, the next decision was to buy a new home that she really liked. Laura had come to the point where she understood that she did not need another person to do things she liked but could start doing them immediately and maybe on the way find a person to love and share her life with.

In the risk of losing yourself

Anna and her husband, John, had been married for three years. This was Anna's second marriage, with her first marriage lasting over 25 years. That first marriage was full of family and career development, but ended after the children were old enough to leave home and begin their adult lives. The lack of compatibility and communication with her former husband and the empty house were such that Anna felt her life would not be fulfilling if they stayed together.

Anna was highly successful in her sales and marketing role, but after her divorce she felt lonely when not working. Even as she tried to enrich her life with travel and new hobbies, she desired a new partner with whom she could share life. She met John when he attended a marketing seminar where she was a presenter. John was interesting, handsome, family oriented, and single. Anna and John began dating and initially found that they had much in common.

Within 18 months of their being together and having an enjoyable and stable relationship, John suggested they get married. As they did get along very well, Anna agreed to it, although she was very hesitant regarding such quick timing. Her intuition said they were moving too fast, but her fear of being alone made her ignore her intuition. While their first couple of years were full of family, friends, and travel, there was something nagging at Anna about the relationship and their communication. In short order, Anna realized that they were far too different. Their lack of common desires and interests was becoming increasingly apparent. Their communication also became very poor. Anna's unhappiness grew to the point of her feeling unhealthy, unhappy, and totally unfulfilled in their relationship. Anna had gotten stuck but did not yet recognize this.

Anna's health and happiness continued to decrease to the point that she knew this was not the relationship for her. In fact, her relationship with John had become harmful to her life as she started to feel depressed and had to take antidepressants. However, she had made a commitment, and she hated hurting anyone's feelings. Anna had already been divorced once, and she feared that people would think less of her. Further, she feared she would not find another relationship in the future. After more months of being depressed and feeling totally stuck, one afternoon she could not get up from her chair at work due to a sudden heavy chest pain. Anna's colleagues feared she had suffered a heart attack and called the ambulance. Fortunately, she had not had a heart attack but a panic attack. This served as a wake-up call for Anna, and she understood she had no other option than to deal with her situation, despite all her fear. As a first step, Anna suggested counseling, which John agreed to. The lack of connection and compatibility with John became more and more evident to Anna as the counseling continued. She finally told John that she could no longer continue the relationship.

Even if it was the right decision for Anna, it was not easy, but after some months she started to feel healthier and could stop taking the antidepressants. Today, two years later, Anna is living a happy life, where she continues working in her chosen field, has developed new interests that she loves, shares a special bond and friendship with a man, and is well on her way to living a life of fulfillment.

These are the tools Anna used:

Deal with your fear: Anna finally understood that she could no longer continue a relationship that made her depressed. She made a choice between a life of promise and her fear of hurting John, her fear of being alone, and worries about what others might think.

➡️ **Make a decision to take a first step:** Anna then made a decision to take a first step. She shared with John that they needed to change their situation and that they needed external help.

➡️ **Resources:** Anna looked for a resource for help. She found a counselor that both she and John could agree upon

➡️ **Discover What You Want:** As part of the counseling, Anna reflected on what really mattered in her life. She had never done that consciously before. Based on this, Anna was able to outline her intentions, her yellow arrows, and understand that the relationship with John was not consistent with her intentions for the short or the longer term.

One day I was alone!

Linda was left by her beloved husband of more than 20 years. Linda felt that they had a great and intimate relationship until one day she discovered that her husband had been cheating on her for more than a year. This was a total shock to her! She never would have suspected this of her wonderful, caring husband, father of their four children. When she found out about his betrayal, things happened quickly. Michael moved out, and Linda was filled with disbelief and sorrow. She had lost her longtime treasured partner! Even worse, he had lied to her for a very long time, which negated her belief in the intimacy that she had thought was so strong between them. Just as significantly, she had lost her given path forward, her yellow arrows that she had believed she could follow for the rest of her life. Soon, their kids would be grown up, which would have given her and Michael much more time to enjoy their time to travel and to grow old together. Suddenly, all of this was gone!

Linda fell down into a deep life crisis. She asked herself if life was even worth living. Over the next weeks, Linda's days were totally dark. She stayed home, missed work, and did only the basic survival activities for her kids and herself. She could not think of anything other than the betrayal of Michael, his new activities, and her lost future. She felt her life had ended, and she couldn't eat.

In the darkest of these times, she received a call from an old friend who had happened to hear about Linda and Michael. This friend had gone through a similar situation, and Linda shared hers. She asked her friend how she had made it through her crisis. Linda also shared her extreme sorrow and feeling of being totally stuck in life. Her friend listened intently and shared various aspects of the healing process she had gone through. Her friend also offered to walk with Linda through this very dark period of her life. Linda agreed.

In their next call, her friend asked Linda if she would try to only think of the present, not the past or the future. She continued by advising Linda to focus only on living each day with her health and her children as her major areas of focus. Linda was doubtful, but she was in such a bad state that she said she would try. Her friend also gave her the book The Power of Now *by Eckhart*

Tolle to read. This book was an eye opener to Linda and was very helpful in keeping her in the "now." Slowly she began to get relief by focusing her life into peaceful moments. She was able to move her mindset to focusing on the present and on the positives of her life.

Within a few months' time, Linda started to feel better and was able to calmly assess her situation. She could more objectively view what had happened and develop some short-term intentions around her life. She was able to see that there was a light at the end of the tunnel and that longer-term planning would be possible. Slowly she started enjoying her wonderful children, her close friends, her network, and the delightful house that she was able to keep.

The Linda of today is a totally new Linda. She did not let herself become a victim of what happened between her and her husband. While she is still processing what happened, her major focus now is on her children and friends and on changing her work life to a much more flexible one. She has begun traveling with friends and has even met a couple of interesting new men. She is now in the process of establishing her longer-term intentions, her yellow arrows. Change was forced upon her, but today Linda can say that she is amazed by how good her life has become.

These are the tools Linda used:

Resources: Linda's first decision was to open herself up to a friend who had gone through a similar crisis.

Resources: She also read the book *The Power of Now* by Eckhart Tolle, and the guidance given in his book helped her cope with her intense pain and sorrow. It also helped her to start refocusing on the present moment and what was good in her life.

Mindset: Linda revised her mindset in view of what had happened to her. Linda was happy in her marriage and thought she and her husband had a wonderful relationship. When she looked back, though, she could see that some parts of the relationship had not been very good. Her husband was very dominant, but for the sake of peace in the family, Linda had managed to overlook this part of their relationship. Now on her own, Linda started to reflect on who she was and what she wanted in life.

Deal with your fear: When Linda's husband unexpectedly left her and her whole world fell apart, she faced and managed one of her biggest fears in life. Having "come out on the other side on her feet" actually made her much stronger and braver than she earlier had been. After this she dared to do things she earlier would not have dared to, like quitting her job and becoming self-employed.

In the chapter "Be Kind to Yourself," we talked about the ability to blossom at any stage in life. Here, we learned how Thomas, Laura, Anna and Linda went through very tough times and decided to seek help, to deal with their fear, and to take a first step. These decisions helped them deal with their situations and ultimately change their lives. Today they all live much more contented, fulfilled, and happy lives, and they all reset their lives to blossom again no matter how difficult a situation seemed. In the next and final chapter, we encourage you to think over your own situation and what you would like to change.

Chapter 5

....

Create Your Own Toolbox

Dear You,

Now you have heard many people's stories and learned about several tools that can help you get unstuck. Perhaps you have the feeling that you know exactly what step or steps you need to take. Or maybe this book so far has given you some new ideas about how you could proceed. This chapter will help you evaluate the tools described, prioritize the ones that are right for you, and then make a plan to start using them. Do this and you will be creating your own toolbox — or the arrows for your life that will help you be more equipped, confident, and energized about your way forward.

Step 1: What is making you feel stuck?

Please write down the issue that you want to change or that is making you feel stuck. Is it a relationship, job, financial, health, attitude, or other issue?

_____

_____

_____

_____

_____

Step 2: What tools will help you deal with your issue?

In Chapter 3 you learned about the 10 different tools. Please check the tools that you have identified as being the right ones for you.

__ 1 Be Kind to Yourself   __ 6 Guilt

__ 2 Mindset   __ 7 Deal with Your Fear

__ 3 Make a Decision to Take a First Step!   __ 8 Find Your Passion

__ 4 Allow Time and Space!   __ 9 Discover What You Want

__ 5 What is Your Excuse?   __ 10 Resources

Step 3: Prioritize the tools you have chosen and start building your own toolbox

Now you can prioritize the tools you want to use. To get the help you need, it's vital to know where to start, and that is why prioritization is important. We suggest you emphasize those tools that will provide you with immediate relief. Then, you can move to goals that will help you assemble a bigger picture or longer-term plan. Write down the tools you have chosen, with 1 being the most important or immediate.

1. _____   6. _____

2. _____   7. _____

3. _____   8. _____

4. _____   9. _____

5. _____   10. _____

Step 4: Give your tools a meaningful, actionable context. Write down a story, based on your chosen tools

You are now on your way to creating your own toolbox. You have identified the tools that will help you change your situation, and you have prioritized them. Now it's important to start thinking of how to use them and to put them into your own context. This is why we strongly recommend you write down your issue and then a story of how you will use your tools to deal with it.

Do the writing automatically. Do not think too long or too much on the text. It's much more important to just write down what comes to your mind based on the tools than to have a perfect and finalized story. This flow in the writing will help your mind create new connections, give you new ideas, and help you fill out parts of your story that are necessary to making a change. Writing your story will help you to put into words what you want and need, and you will be able to communicate to others and maybe get unexpected help and speed to do the steps.

An example for illustration:

Identified issue:

I am stuck in my negative thoughts about myself and am also doubting the relationship I am in.

Chosen tools:

Be kind to yourself, deal with your fear, and use resources.

Example of a story based on my identified issue and chosen tools:

*I am very frustrated with my thoughts about myself and my abilities to change my situation. I am not happy in my relationship anymore but do not know what to do about it. When reading this book, I have understood that I am too hard on myself, so the first step for me is to start paying attention to my self-talk. I want to become **kind to myself** and start building a more positive attitude towards myself and my abilities to change.*

*I was inspired by the **resources** section and will invite a few close friends to help and challenge me about my relationship. Until now I have not actively dealt with my doubts about it. I have been hiding behind my **fears** of being alone, having to start new, and not knowing where to start, but now I have come to realize that I will not be able to change my partner and that I have to change or make a change, despite the things I fear.*

I know that by focusing on being kind to myself and daring to open up to my friends with my problems, I will be able to connect with them in a new, more vulnerable, and real way. I believe that by doing so, they will better understand me and will provide the support, challenge, and inspiration I need to start making changes to my life.

_____

_____

_____

_____

_____

_____

_____

_____

_____

_____

Congratulations on having taken this important step towards changing your situation! You have identified your issue, found tools that will help you alter your situation, and also laid out a plan for how to use the tools. Having a clear path forward with distinct arrows that help to point out the direction you want to go is an important milestone. This will help you to begin your new path. You have now created your first story in writing. This was a first great step. Soon you will be living your new story and your new life!

That is wonderful!

Concluding Words

When we told a friend that we were writing a book about being stuck, he asked, *"What? Why? You have never been stuck!"* This is not correct. Our experience is that everybody gets stuck at some point in their lives. We, both Terry and Nina, have been stuck several times, as you might have recognized in this book. What's most important is not how many times or where we were stuck, but how we managed to get into a new phase in life, using the different tools presented in this book. We both feel compassion and respect for the times in life when we were stuck, since those times formed us into the people we are today.

We hope that sharing our experiences, thoughts, and discoveries will help you find the tools to create, clarify, and then follow the yellow arrows toward your chosen direction in life. If you find that you are unable to see the arrows you developed, then it's time to stop, reflect, and refine your direction so the arrows can again become clear.

We wish you a wonderful journey in exploring life and creating your new future!

References

Singer, Michael A. *The Untethered Soul.* Oakland, CA: New Harbinger Publications/Noetic Books, 2007.

Tolle, Eckhart. *The Power of Now.* Vancouver, BC: Namaste Publishing, Inc., 1999/2004.

About the Authors

Nina Engstrand was born in Finland and has lived in Stockholm, Sweden since 1995.

Nina started her career as a language teacher and then moved to service sales, education, and partner management positions in the global IT industry. In 2017, Nina started her own coaching practice and co-developed an app for personal growth. Nina holds a master of science degree from Åbo Akademi, Finland, and an executive MBA from the Stockholm School of Economics. Nina loves outdoor life, reading, personal development, cafes, and travelling.

Terry Belmont was born and lives in California, USA. He has over 30 years of experience in leading large, complex healthcare organisations. In his role as a CEO Terry has coached and mentored many individuals in various positions and continues to do so today. Terry is currently Chair of the Board of an international NASDAQ listed company as well as having other board and strategic advisory roles. He holds a bachelor of science degree in business from University of Redlands and a masters degree in healthcare management from University of California, Berkeley. Besides his passion for healthcare and supporting personal development, Terry loves varied outdoor activities, world travel, music, and being with friends.

Sending You Gratitude

Thank You so much for buying this book. As an expression of our gratitude, we would like to offer you "10 tips to raise your energy when feeling low" to download for FREE.

To Download:

theinvitationtochange.com/download

CPSIA information can be obtained
at www.ICGtesting.com
Printed in the USA
BVOW06s2133211117
501048BV00009B/190/P